SO-AXA-487

CULTURE SHOCK!
Indonesia

Cathie Draine
& Barbara Hall

TIMES BOOKS INTERNATIONAL
Singapore • Kuala Lumpur

The spelling of Bahasa Indonesia in this book is
in accordance with the recommendations of
MABBIM, Majlis Bahasa Brunei Indonesia
Malaysia

Illustrations by Bernard Napitupulu
Photographs by courtesy of the *Jakarta Post*
Cover photographs by Wendy Chan

This book is published by
Times Books International,
an imprint of Times Editions Pte Ltd
Times Centre, 1 New Industrial Road
Singapore 1953
2nd Floor, Wisma Hong Leong Yamaha
50 Jalan Penchala, 46050 Petaling Jaya
Selangor, Malaysia

Second edition 1990

Printed by Jin Jin Printing Industry Pte Ltd

ISBN 981 204 158 3

The Indonesian expression of thanks,
terima kasih, literally means
'We have received your love.'

The expression of acknowledgement,
terima kasih kembali, literally means
'The love we have received, we now return.'

You hold in your hands a manifestation of both
the love we have received from Indonesia and her people
and that love which now we pass to you.

CONTENTS

FOREWORD

Indonesia has been welcoming guests for centuries. The beauty and wealth of the country, the charm of the people and the fascination of the many cultures have drawn the curious, the studious and the businessman. However, when Marco Polo visited in the 13th century, he did not bring his family; the contemporary businessman does.

Culture Shock Indonesia is a positive, useful tool that will help build cultural bridges with understanding and a lot of practical information. It is a welcome travel companion and an essential aid to the foreigner establishing his home here.

We extend our welcome—*Selamat Datang!*—and the invitation to become participants in our rich culture and friendly way of life.

Joop Ave
Director General of Tourism, Indonesia

INTRODUCTION

Culture Shock Indonesia divides itself into two pertinent topics, culture shock and Indonesia.

Culture shock is a function of people's recent ability to travel vast distances quickly. Centuries ago, voyagers complained about endless dreary days at sea and meagre food. When they encountered new lands, food and customs they were generally positive and uncritical. Traders who traversed Asia and India on lurching camels rarely utilised negative comparisons between 'life here' and 'life back there'. The very slowness of travel took the sharp edge off the shock of the unfamiliar, the untasted, the unexperienced.

Contemporary travellers are 'shocked' by the sudden juxtaposition of things new and strange with situations remembered and familiar. We suggest that culture shock is a continuum of adjusting to changing conditions, including the process of re-entry to your original culture.

Indonesia is where we find ourselves—working, living, raising families, exploring. It was necessary and difficult to limit the areas and ethnic groups discussed to those where most expatriates are sent—Java, Sumatra, Bali and Sulawesi. We are painfully aware that this choice excludes half the land and people of the archipelago—the beautiful and fascinating Nusa Tenggara.

Culture Shock Indonesia offers practical insights which were gathered broadly from the international community and our many Indonesian friends. Our goal was to provide information and background to help each of you construct a positive outlook and an ability to function comfortably. Thus you will find a brief history and description of the more familiar ethnic groups, and fact, examples, vocabulary and words to say that will help you function in society, your office and home.

Recognising that expatriates are scattered throughout the islands, information from surveys on living conditions in the provinces is included. Some of the aspects of culture shock that one can predictably encounter in Indonesia are described and examined. We offer some solid suggestions to ease the process of re-entry into the home culture and to assuage the desperate moments of culture shock relapse!

We hope that *Culture Shock Indonesia* will smoothen your way a little, brighten each day and give you tools for fashioning a comfortable adjustment here.

Cathie Draine   Jakarta, Indonesia
Barbara Hall   16 February 1986

TERIMA KASIH

How can we ever say 'Thank You' to the hundreds whose knowledge, experience, concern, hours of assistance and unmeasured love and support are on the pages of *Culture Shock Indonesia*? We accept it all as a demonstration of *gotong royong* (working together), a term that has new meaning for us. We hope you will recognise the adventures, personal discoveries, suggestions and enthusiasm each of you gave to the book.

Our many Indonesian friends have shared their opinions, experiences, time and interest. You have opened new opportunities for understanding to us. We are deeply grateful for the fruits of those friendships. Several hundred families we have worked with in the Comprehensive Orientation Programme of the Indonesian Community Activity Centre and the Canadian International Development Agency in-country briefing programmes taught us a great deal about the newcomer's point of view. Our long-stayer friends from many nations provided a sense of balance and reminded us of the value of humour. Thank you.

We would like to list each person who added to the book. Your names we keep in our hearts. We acknowledge the assistance of many persons in the management of Atlantic Richfield Indonesia Inc., the staff of the Jakarta International School Library, and the *Jakarta Post* for the photographs.

We are grateful to Mr Joop Ave, Director General of Tourism, Indonesia, for providing the Foreword. For consistently encouraging words from David Hall ('Of course you can do it') and LeRoy Draine ('I don't see an immediate problem'), we say *'Terima kasih banyak, Tuan-Tuan* for your enthusiasm, support ... and for bringing us here in the first place!

The energy and aspirations of Indonesia's young people are a great resource.

Chapter One

UNITY IN DIVERSITY

The travel books do a great job of telling you what you are going to see in Indonesia. The purpose of this book and this first chapter is to acquaint you with some of the things you are going to feel. We are not talking about hot and sweaty feelings; we are talking about the pulse of the country, the deep, prideful feelings of nationalism, the strength that is found within one's *suku* (ethnic group) and within the framework of the nation.

Consider this first chapter your very necessary homework. Then, we 'hit the streets', begin our exploration with some data from history and become part of the street scene.

MERDEKA! FREEDOM!

In 40 years—little more than one generation—the modern nation of Indonesia has been created. That accounts for much of the exuberance, enthusiasm, nationalistic pride and the sense of accomplishment that the people feel toward their country.

The Stirrings of Nationalism

The hoped-for nation was scattered as islands across several inland seas. As the people struggled for freedom and unity it may have seemed that the odds were against them.

The members of the Youth Congress, in the 'Youth Oath' (*Sumpah Pemuda*) in 1928, marked a commitment to independence and a direction to the energy to be found in unity. They proposed *satu nusa* (one country); *satu bangsa* (one people); and *satu bahasa* (one language).

Tanah Air Kita (Our Land and Water)

The archipelago called *tanah air*, which literally means 'land and water' but is understood as 'fatherland', is as big as Australia, and larger than China or the United States; the land area alone is approximately one-third of Europe (excluding Russia).

Former Vice-President Hatta wrote in 1953: 'Nature has ordained that Indonesia, lying between two continents—the Asian mainland and Australia—and washed by the waters of two vast oceans (the Indian and the Pacific) must maintain intercourse with lands stretching in a great circle around it.' This statement has become an ideological commitment nourished by Indonesia's activity in ASEAN (Association of Southeast Asian Nations) affairs.

Islands

The more than 6000 inhabited islands of the world's largest island complex are usually grouped: the Greater Sundas (Sumatra, Java, Kalimantan and Sulawesi); the Lesser Sundas (the chain from Bali

The challenge is to include as many as possible in the drive for development.

to Timor, also known as Nusa Tenggara); and the Moluccas (extending north of the Lesser Sundas and east of Sulawesi).

Java, Bali and Sumatra are the 'inner islands'. Java is the most fertile of the islands and supports almost 60 per cent of the population. It is an island of farmers in small villages who continue to produce the rice, rubber, coffee, tea, sugar and tobacco that have brought centuries of wealth. The capital city, Jakarta, is located on Java's

north coast and more or less sets the business and social standards for the country. Sumatra is the third largest of the Indonesian islands, with approximately a quarter the country's total land area.

New Guinea (Irian Jaya) and Kalimantan are the second and third largest islands in the world. Kalimantan is swamps, dense forest, wandering rivers and few people—less than 6 persons per square kilometre.

SULU SEA

SULAWESI SEA

PACIFIC OCEAN

Menado

MALUKU SEA

NORTH SULAWESI

arinda

Palu

CENTRAL SULAWESI

Straits of Makassar

SOUTH SULAWESI

SOUTHEAST SULAWESI

SERAM SEA

g Padang

Kendari

Ambon

MALUKU

IRIAN JAYA

BANDA SEA

FLORES SEA

EAST NUSA TENGGARA

ARAFURA SEA

WEST USA TENGGARA

SAWU SEA

Dilli

TIMOR

Kupang

TIMOR SEA

INDONESIA

Population

Indonesia's population—over 153 million—of Arabs, Chinese, Pakistanis, Indians, Europeans and Eurasians plus the native Indonesians—makes the country the fifth most populous in the world. They speak between 250 and 400 languages or regional dialects.

It is a nation of villagers. The 27 political provinces rapidly shatter into an astonishing five-digit number of villages—61,341 of them that contain almost 90 per cent of the population. Of the total population, 30 per cent own 71 per cent of the land; 46 per cent own only 12 per cent of the land.

BUILDING THE NATION

The Indonesian personality has long absorbed foreign cultural influences and converted them into something indigenous. The *Ramayana* and the *Mahabharata*, for example, breathe life into the *wayang* puppet performances and provide moral comment and guidance for the individual.

The builders of the nation acknowledged this practice of absorbing ideas and then looked for elements of 'Indonesian-ness'. They found the new nation heir to two significant legacies.

First, they affirmed the presence of a typically Indonesian spirit, personality and way of doing things that has its roots in the past. This view owes much to the elegant and sophisticated Golden Age of the Majapahit Empire in the 14th century (1293–1389).

Second, they drew from the feeling of cooperative harmony, the tradition of decision by consensus (*musyawarah mufakat*) and the long-established pattern of mutual assistance, *gotong-royong*, in the accomplishment of economic tasks.

Years later, President Suharto would reaffirm this blend of strength: 'In our culture harmony is regarded as the most essential value: the problem is not to destroy traditional values but to adjust them to the demands of development.'

The Indonesian citizen is very aware of these values in the modern world, reshaped as the tools of nationalism. The *selamatan* remains as the prayerful ceremony invoked by President and peasant alike. *Gotong-royong* is invoked to inspire a feeling of togetherness in the office as well as in the field.

Nationalism

The third *sila* of the *Pancasila* (see *Pancasila* in 'Indonesian Perceptions') includes the concept of nationalism. The people are encouraged to be Indonesian first, and a member of their *sukubangsa* (ethnic group) second.

QUALITY OF LIFE

One of the promises of unity was a piece of the good life for all. Life expectancy has risen to age 50. Well over a third of the population is under 20, making Indonesia almost a nation of young people.

Indonesia is no longer classed as an underdeveloped country. Literacy rates are almost 75% country-wide at all age levels and over 700,000 students are in institutions of higher learning. *Puskesmas*, public health centres, are visible in the villages. Increased emphasis is being put on 'well-baby' clinics. Family planning (*keluarga berencana*) is a national concern.

However, only 12% of the people have access to clean water. Over 60% of the children die before they are five. Too often one reads of villagers relying on traditional treatment before failing results prompt them to send their sick babies to the health centre where it is often too late to save them.

MEETING THE MAJOR ETHNIC GROUPS

Where to begin? Burdened by staggering statistics that delineate differences—over 300 ethnic groups, cultures ranging from Stone Age to high-tech, geography from desert to snow peaks and all in between—the foreigner gropes for a starting point to meet the

17

Indonesians. For the newcomer, much seems strange. One is dazzled by the tales of the *koteka*-clad, Stone Age Dani tribesman from Irian Jaya but the chance of meeting, for instance, a nude Baliem Valley male wearing a gourd penis sheath at a dinner party is slim. Not impossible, but slim. The tales of the headhunters of Kalimantan (Borneo) are chilling ... and history. While much of the exotic is truly here, we must come to grips with people we live next to, share office space with.

Superficial ethnic generalisations lead to Cocktail Party Comparisons: '... all Bataks play guitars and sing in restaurants; all Balinese carve statues and dance; all Javanese giggle when they are sad.' Not true, of course, but where does one start?

The answer is: with facts. Here is information about some of the most commonly encountered ethnic groups. It is data that the Indonesians assume you will or should know, plus some clues that will help you identify an individual's ethnic group by his personal name. The material is not intended as comparisons nor is it complete. It points to the important aspects of each group's culture to provide a path of knowledge for the newcomer.

Consider this information as seeds to plant in your social garden, simple tools to aid you in becoming educated about Indonesia and the Indonesians. It is difficult not to become fascinated.

Achenese

Centuries of intermarriage with Bataks, Hindus, Javanese, Dravidians, Arabs, Chinese and Niasan slaves have produced people usually tall, slim and almost Caucasoid in appearance.

For various reasons, Acheh in northernmost Sumatra was in rebellion until 1961, when it became a province of Indonesia. It had been a trading state for more than a thousand years and was one of the first contact points of Islam in Indonesia.

Traditional Achenese villages are in the middle of rice fields, heavily sheltered by trees. Achenese are essentially agriculturists,

fine metal workers, weavers, potters and boat builders.

Marriage is in accord with the rules of Islam; divorce and remarriage are common and *adat* (traditional law) has great influence. Islam is strong but exists alongside a 'heretical, pantheistic mysticism'; magic is significant in agricultural practice, interpretation of dreams is widespread and sickness is attributed to evil spirits and cured by magic. Personal names tend to sound Arabic.

Badui

These isolated and mysterious people live in 35 small villages in West Java. The families of the three 'inner' villages consider themselves the descendants of gods and have little to do with the outside world. The 'outer' villages and their inhabitants are slightly more accessible. The Badui call themselves Orang Kanekes (Kanakes is the name of their sacred territory) or Orang Parahiang (the name of a mythological kingdom inhabited by spirits). It is speculated that they fled the Muslim Bantamese in 1579 as refugees of the ancient kingdom of Pajajaran. Even now, the Badui appear not to be interested in the outside world.

They have an elaborate mythology with spirits and deities, many

of which retain Hindu names. Writing is generally considered taboo because of the magic power thought to be associated with it. Inscribed bamboo sticks are used in ceremonies. The markings on these are thought to be the remnants of an indigenous script.

The Badui are 'slash and burn' agriculturists and hunters. Most of their religious rituals are associated with the harvest. They are known as the pickers and gatherers of durian during the fruit's season.

Balinese

For many, the island of Bali evokes visions of paradise: volcanoes, pounding surf, rippling terraced rice fields and a rich spiritual life.

Bali has seen increasing political activity and tourism development since 1950. Influenced by (8th–11th centuries) and then by Hindu Java (11th–15th centuries), the Balinese retained the appearance of Hindu ritual and drama more than the Hindu philosophy and mysticism. A typical village residence is high-walled and contains the home, several courtyards and small family shrines. Each village tends to support a specific craft; for example, Ubud is the village of painters and Mas the village of carvers.

The villages are highly organised in relation to land ownership and land use. Wet rice culture with sophisticated irrigation is practised. Within the villages, each kin group is united by the notion

of descent from a single and impersonal ultimate genetic source, a deity, or a physical location. Status in Bali is commonly reflected in the names. (See 'Indonesian Perceptions, Names'.)

Balinese religion is 'the religion of water' or *agama tirta*. The water is blessed by the Brahmana priest and used in the ceremonies. Each temple has its festival (every 210 days if it observes the Balinese calendar and every 365 if it observes the Gregorian calendar) which involves food, music, dance (sometimes trance dancing), prayers and the sprinkling of holy water.

Many tourists are familiar with the masks and the dance drama of the witch, Rangda, and dragon, Barong—characters in the ceremony associated with the death temple and the *adat desa* (law of the village).

The Balinese believe that illness is caused by spirits and healed by magic in seance. The release of the soul after death is finalised in extravagant cremation ceremonies.

Batak

Anthropologists consider this group from the interior of north-central Sumatra a model of all ancient proto-Malay cultures of the Indonesian archipelago. The Batak's former reputation for

cannibalism is based on *adat* or the enforcement of traditional law. Their hero ancestor is Si Radja Batak, born of supernatural parentage on a holy rock near Lake Toba. Within the last 150 years, they were heavily influenced by the Rheinische Mission; the largest Christian group is around Lake Toba.

Batak houses are distinctive, with a trapdoor in the floor, large gable ends and carved buffalo horns. The wood carving and weaving, especially the *ulos* scarves, are well known.

They are a proud people with volatile tempers. Many of their famous singers are known beyond Sumatra as entertainers. Young Bataks court each other with poetry contests and observe complicated marriage *adat* or traditions.

The Toba word for village, *huta*, appears in many of the family names. Common names are Sinaga, Simatupang, Silitonga, Pangabean, Hutapea, Simanjuntak, Hutasoit, Sembiring, Lubis, Nasution and Tobing.

Bugis

These 'boat people', long known as Sea Gypsies, were widely scattered in the estuaries and offshore islands off the north and east coasts of Kalimantan and Sulawesi. They are thought by many to be the same ethnic stock as the inland Toradjanese. They may be

Bernard T.H. Ngantupulu '85

disappearing as an ethnic group as they settle and become more assimilated. They have a history as traders, pirates, and coastal colonisers. They were early followers of Islam.

Foreign residents usually associate the Bugis with the colourful wind-driven boats anchored in the harbour at Sunda Kelapa on Java and sailed as cargo boats to the eastern islands. Almost as well known is one of their cottage industries producing high quality silk that is eagerly sought after by residents and visitors. Andi as a male first name hints at Bugis lineage and is a title of rank.

Dayak

The name of the specific ethnic group, Dayaks, is generally given to describe any of the many small groups of people who live along the rivers of inland Kalimantan. Broadly speaking, these are groups of non-Muslims who live in relatively permanent settlements, practise a system of shifting cultivation and still hunt and fish using the spear and blowpipe.

The Dayaks have extremely complicated sex and marriage beliefs and taboos, in addition to active belief in ancestral spirits and spirits resident in trees, rocks, water and plants. Shamans—usually old women—function as caretakers of the community's mental and physical health.

The Dayaks have a rich tradition of art, featuring wood and bamboo carving, tatooing, weaving and beadwork, and basket and mat plaiting. In some areas they have become skilled metal workers.

Javanese

Jawa, the Javanese name for themselves, comes from the Sanskrit, *yawa* (barley). Two-thirds of the national population live on the island of Java. The villages are small; each contains from 300 to 3000 people. The buildings are clustered in groves of trees and appear as islands in the sea of fields. The villagers practise wet rice farming in small, highly fragmented land holdings; the majority of peasants are landless agricultural labourers.

There is a literary history in the Javanese language dating from the 11th century. Two Javanese words you are sure to meet are *pendopo*, the large open formal pavilion seen in traditional upper class houses and commonly in government buildings in Java; and *priyayi*, a word synonymous with government officials and civil service employees today. In the past the term referred to the early nationalists who worked for independence.

Modern spoken Javanese uses nine levels reflecting rank, status, age and degree of acquaintance between speakers. Even family

names reflect social importance (older, younger), rather than sex (brother, sister).

The Javanese have developed *batik* to an art form, refined the playing of the *gamelan*, and incorporated the shadow play of India into the ethical system as *wayang kulit*.

Javanese often have only one name, and upper class persons will

choose a family name. Common family names often end in 'o': Subroto, Suharto, Sukarno, Widodo, Sartono, Sumantono, Hadikusomo, Sosroamijoyo, Suryopranoto, Pusposufondo and Suhardjono.

Minahasa

Now a largely Eurasian population in the northern part of Sulawesi, the Minahasa are an agricultural people. They believe their original ancestor, Liminu'ut, the god of earth, was born from a stone and then

25

married her son, To'ar, the sun god. They are almost totally Christianised and socialised by the Dutch. Few *adat* inhibitions remain. Feasts and large gatherings are common among

the Minahasa and westerners usually feel comfortable around them.

Typical family names are Lantang, Kawilarang, Gerungan, Rumantir, Mantik, Wowor, Pontoh, Wowungan and Mogot.

Minangkabau

These Muslims from the highlands of west-central Sumatra are usually associated with Padang, their provincial capital. There are archaeological links with the Hindu kingdom of Majapahit and heavy Dutch influence in the 19th century. The Minangkabau were active in both the Indonesian revolution and the present government.

A typical large Minangkabau house has a curved sweeping roof resembling buffalo horns. Their society is matrilineal and the women

control the house. Divorce and remarriage are common.

The Minangkabau believe in a large group of supernaturals and spirits and also that 'Heaven is below the sole of the mother's foot,' i.e., a person cannot go to Heaven if he mistreats his mother.

Minangkabau names com-

monly sound Islamic. Personal names often have the letter 'z', as in Herliza, Faizal, Rizal, Gozali and Armizal.

Overseas Chinese

This largest and most important alien group in Indonesia is found chiefly in the port cities. The largest concentrations are in Java, eastern Sumatra and western Kalimantan.

Chinese have been in Indonesia for centuries. Many single Hakka and Hokkien males came in response to the Dutch policy of recruiting alien labour for plantations and mines in the latter half of the 19th century, and were encouraged by the Dutch to move into middle-level commercial and financial positions. Chinese women were allowed to emigrate to Indonesia in the early 20th century.

The modern definition of 'Chinese' for census purposes remains difficult: the *peranakan* Chinese tend to be assimilated and identify their future with that of Indonesia while *totok* Chinese tend to be less assimilated and more China-oriented.

Sundanese

Their home in the Priangan Highlands of West Java is called 'land of *parahyangan*' (paradise). In his book, *History of Java*, Sir Stamford Raffles speaks of the Highlands as a centre of Dutch controlled forced coffee cultivation in the 19th century.

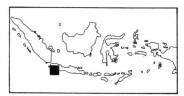

27

The Sundanese share not only the island but also some ceremonies and arts with the Javanese. For example, the Sundanese wedding is also an elaborate and gracious affair; *wayang golek* (wooden puppets) are the Sundanese adaptation of the *wayang kulit* or leather puppets; and the *suling* or flute is as associated with the Sundanese as the *gamelan* is with the Javanese.

Magic and sorcery are important at all levels of Sundanese life. The Sundanese believe, for example, that people who die in disgrace become roaming malevolent spirits.

Common family names tend to end in 'a': Nataatmaja, Tirtakusuma, Kusumaatmaja. Common first names also end in 'a': Suhanda, Suhanya and Juanda. Nicknames are Ujang, Iim, Juju, Ucup and Dadang.

Toradjanese

These 'men of the mountain' from the rugged areas of central Sulawesi are hunters, carvers and makers of bark cloth. Buffalo and buffalo horns are their status symbols and buffalo is given as the bride price. Funerals are major events for the family and very special tourist attractions. Their dead are placed in the limestone cliffs and effigies of the dead are left in 'porches' in the cliffs.

The southern tribes believe they came to the island in canoes, *lembang*. Their houses reflect the form of the boats.

Chapter Two

THE STREET SCENE

It is probably too much to expect that anyone caught in a traffic jam can think sublime thoughts about the mystical prince for whom the street is named.

However, it is this incredible exercise in contrast, this Asian *yin* and *yang*, this sense of ridiculous and sublime in meeting and honking and snarling at each other on the street that brings such zest to living here.

This chapter hopes to illuminate some of the characters that animate the street names and the streets themselves. *Selamat jalan!* Happy travelling!

STREETS: A BRIEF LESSON

Throughout Indonesia many of the streets are named for the heroes that all Indonesia honours. Familiarity with these will give you an appreciation for the men of Indonesia's history and be grist for your conversational mill. You could also charm an Indonesian friend with your knowledge. Street names are in capitals.

Kings and Kingdoms

From the 6th to the 10th centuries most of the names honour kings and kingdoms. PURNAWARMAN was the first Hindu ruler on Java. In AD 500 his kingdom, Taruma Negara, stretched from Jakarta to Bogor. SRIWIJAYA (600–1378) names a kingdom in South Sumatra active in maritime affairs, prominent in economics and a centre for Buddhist learning. The kingdom was destroyed by the rulers of Java. In modern Indonesia the memory lingers that Sumatra was once the rival of Java.

Both SHAILENDRA and DAKSA are the names associated with the 'Kings of the Mountain', thought to be from Cambodia. They were rulers of a Hindu-influenced kingdom in Central Java (759–900), and were best known for creating the temple complex at Prambanan.

AIRLANGGA and his father-in-law DARMAWANGSA are associated with the Kediri Dynasty (1135) of East Java. Airlangga was half Balinese, a mystic, and an aesthete. Because most of the facts of his life have passed into legend, he is often referred to as the Indonesian King Arthur.

The Majapahit Empire

From the 10th to the 16th centuries most of the names centre around the incredible MAJAPAHIT Empire whose accomplishments still feed the sense of Indonesian identity.

While Europe was caught in the burst of world awareness of the Middle Ages, Indonesia was seeing great Hindu kingdoms rise and fall, other Hindu kingdoms shrivel in significance, and great merchant and intellectual intercourse with China. This was the beginning of contact with European explorers and traders.

The Majapahit kingdom, though begun on Java, grew in 1293–1500 to encompass almost as much land as modern Indonesia. It strove for national unification and the development of a national identity. During the struggle for Indonesia's independence from colonial rule, it was the reality of the Majapahit Empire that fuelled the dreams of the freedom fighters. WIJAYA was the founder of the Empire and the first king.

The names HAYAM WURUK, PRAPANCA and GAJAH MADAH are related even though the first was the greatest of the rulers, the second a hermit poet writing under a pseudonym, and the third a ruthless but efficient prime minister.

Prapanca, writing in his cave, produced an original national work, the *Nagarakertagama*, in 1306, glorifying Hayam Wuruk. Fortunately for today's letter writer, anyone living on Jalan Hayam Wuruk does not have to use the full name, Dyah Hayam Wuruk Sri Rajasanagara. Gajah Madah, through power and diplomacy, was directly responsible for the expansion of the Majapahit Empire. He uttered the famous Palapa Vow (*Sumpah Palapa*), 'I will not retire before the conquest of the entire *nusantara* is completed ... Irian Jaya ... Bali ... Kalimantan ... Sunda ... Palembang ... Only after the conquest of these lands will I retire.' In recognition of the value of communication in unification, modern Indonesians named their satellite communication system, Palapa.

SANG ADITIAWARMAN, a much travelled diplomat of the Majapahit courts, went to Sumatra and founded the Malayapura kingdom in Minangkabau. BRAWIJAYA and his most famous son RADEN PATAH mark a moment of movement from Hinduism to Islam in the Majapahit era. Although the son of a royal Hindu father, Raden Patah accepted Islam, became a student of SUNAN NGAMPEL, and then founded the Islamic state of Demak in north

Java. Sunan Ngampel is also known as RADEN REHMAT and Bong Swee Ho. The Muslim community he founded in Surabaya is generally acknowledged as the first on Java.

Meanwhile, Raden Patah added the name SENOPATI, meaning 'prime minister', after he and his Islamic armies defeated the Hindu-Buddhist armies of his father. Raden Patah's full name was Senopati Jimbun Ngabdurrahmon Panembahan Palembang Saidin Pantagama. One is grateful not to have *that* as a street address!

The Malacca Straits

In the 15th century several men from the Malacca Straits gave their names to history. ISKANDAR SYAH founded the kingdom of Malacca. HANG TUAH, HANG JEBAT, HANG LEKIR, HANG LEKIU were naval heroes whose deeds are immortalised in the *Sejarah Melayu*, a Malay literary classic. *Hang* before a name is rendered as a title, as in Sir for knights.

Two rulers sallied forth from Demak in the early 1500s to do battle with the Portuguese. PATIUNUS, the son of Raden Patah, was unsuccessful but FATAHILLAH conquered Sunda Kelapa, the old port of Jakarta. The Jakarta City Museum bears his name.

MATARAM gave its name to two kingdoms on Java. In the 9th century the SENJAYA family founded the first dynasty. The second kingdom of Mataram gives us SULTAN AGUNG, who codified *adat* (tradition) and Muslim law. PAKUBUWONO was the name given to the courts at Yogyakarta and Solo, created by the Dutch in a successful attempt to break and decentralise the power of the second Mataram kingdom.

The New Nation

From the 17th century on, the names are those of the builders of the new nation of Indonesia, the resistance fighters, agitators for nationhood, and pragmatic politicians.

Indonesian leaders throughout the islands struggled with the

Dutch presence for over 300 years. HASANUDDIN fought in Sulawesi in the mid-17th century. In the early 1800s TUANKU IMAM BONJOL led the Minangkabau resistance in Sumatra and Prince DIPONEGORO and his adviser, KYAI MAJA, were active in Central Java in the Java Rebellion (1826).

In the 20th century, TEUKU UMAR was an Achenese warrior and SISINGAMANGARAJA XII a Batak resistance leader. DR. CIPTO MANGUNKUSUMO was in exile for most of his adult life. Jakarta's largest public hospital is named for him. JENDERAL SUDIRMAN is almost a folk hero for leading his troops in the final moments of the war for independence, even though he was dying of tuberculosis.

Three men are always linked with the awakening of national consciousness and the Sarekat Islam, the first mass political group in Indonesia. They are the Javanese COKROAMINOTO, an early friend of Sukarno and often regarded as the 'grandfather' of Indonesian independence, the Sumatran ABDUL MUIS, a writer, and HAJI AGUS SALIM, a political figure.

The six generals and one captain killed on the night of 30 September 1965 in the attempted communist coup, are honoured by street names in nearly every city. It would be appropriate to recognise them: JENDERAL A. YANI, LET. JENDERAL S. PARMAN, KAPTEN TENDEAN, LET. JENDERAL HARYONO, LET. JENDERAL PANJAITAN, BRIG. JENDERAL SUTOYO, LET. JENDERAL SOEPRAPTO.

Indonesians seem reluctant to name streets after a living person, but we do see the names of recent political figures such as HAJI MOHD. HATTA, SULTAN SJAHRIR, DR. IG. JUANDA, and DR. SAM RATULANGI, who were all prominent in the activities of the early cabinets of the new republic.

You will note that it is common for a street to change its name usually at an intersection. For example, in Jakarta, Jalan Gunung

Sahari in the northern part of the city becomes Jalan Pasar Senen, Jalan Kramat Raya, Jalan Salemba, and Jalan Mataram Raya as it proceeds south. Not to be outdone, one of the main streets in Surabaya enters from the west as Jalan Gresik and then becomes Jalan Rajawali, Kemb. Jepun, Jalan Kapasan and Jalan Keneran on its way to the beach in the east of the city.

Rather than try to impose a system of logic on this, consider that until recently store numbers were more perfidious personal choice (favourite or lucky numbers) than a precise method of location. So knowing the various names of some of the long arteries helps you locate a place.

Streets will get renamed periodically. No one quite understands why. Perhaps it is an opportunity to 'pass around' the streets to honour various individuals. In these situations the Indonesian tendency is to say: 'Jalan Sabang? Ah, I always call it ...' and refer to the old name!

WHAT'S IN A STREET?

A subject sure to provoke an impassioned outburst of emotion in the hearts (and mouths) of most expatriates is the subject of streets and roads. The westerner will probably mutter that the roads are cluttered, inefficient, confusing, poorly maintained, vaguely marked, scary, venues for all manner of shops-on-wheels—and only by the way does there seem to be any provision for cars and trucks!

The Indonesian generally views the roadways as wonderful badminton and volleyball courts, extensions of everyone's stores, pasturage for sheep, geese, chickens and goats, a reasonable extension of the *kampung*, probably biodegradable, a public area for drying crops, placing offerings, disposing of rats and snakes, a broad avenue for schoolchildren to walk six to eight abreast, a fine area for teaching very young children to cycle—and only recently a logical place for cars and trucks.

It is probably oversimplifying it to suggest that motorised vehicles have staked their claims to the roads only within the last generation. However, to check this hypothesis, one has only to journey off the main roads. At almost every city limit the motorable roads give way to foot traffic.

Street Noise

Street noise is commercial rather than vehicular: *saPUUUUU!* calls the broom and brush man; *spatTTUUUUU!* notifies the shoe repairman; *NYAK! NYAK!* barks the cooking oil seller; *AAOOOO!* carols the fish peddler.

The Rhythm of the Streets

The streets never sleep. Persons who shuffle down the roads to the mosque to pray in the pre-dawn give way to athletes in training and they give way to the buses and trucks that claim the roads in clouds of foul exhaust. Roosters gargle and scream their salutes to the sun as they lead their ladies to the roadsides to scratch for food.

By midday, the streets belong to the women who cluster at house gates exchanging gossip, chatting with friends returning from the market, selling bottles and newspapers and watching benignly their children playing along the edge of the roads. The occasional garbage picker comes by with his wagon full of plastic pieces, folded cardboard, bottles and bundled newspapers.

Flocks of uniformly dressed schoolchildren seem always on the streets. Classes run from 7 a.m. to 12:30 and again from 1 p.m. to 5:30.

As the sun falls, the foodstalls appear and attract their customers who eat, then stay to chat and watch each other watching each other!

So much seems temporary or at least movable about the streets, one almost overlooks the non-movable ice storage boxes, the *tambal ban* tyre repair, the street barbers who usually set up shop under large trees, the little cigarette and candy wagons, the car oil vendors, the garbage dump sites and their contrast—the plant nurseries.

35

The Expatriate Attitude

The typical raised-on-the-Autobahn or used-to-the-Interstate expatriate snarls as traffic lights quit functioning and cars, buses, bicycles, motorcycles, and all manner of wagons-to-pull and wagons-to-push line up nose to nose at the intersection and dare each other to move.

It takes a short time for some basic traffic truths to become manifest. One expatriate, Dick Sturgis, attempted to categorise and contain the chaos in a wonderful personal essay that he circulated in the expatriate community, 'The Flow, Pick, Big, No-See-Chicken Simplified System for Successful Driving in Asia'.

Flow: It does not matter how many white lines are painted on the road or how many lanes of traffic there should be—go with the flow. Mr Sturgis recalls 'flowing' in eight lanes of traffic all going in one direction on a four-lane, two-way traffic street.

The only real victims are the street sign and he patience of the drivers!

Small boys appear quickly to push vehicles, large and small, through the floods that come with the rainy season.

Pick: The basic principle of 'pick' is, whoever can place a portion of his vehicle in front of the other has achieved the right of way. Because all Indonesians are aware of this, there is incredible squeezing and jostling and pushing for position at crossroads.

Big: This is easy. Size rules. As you master the principles of 'flowing' and 'picking' you can compete more equally. When in doubt, however, size wins. Be especially gracious when dealing with garbage trucks and let someone else get immediately behind them.

No-See-Chicken: This is the great game of dare played with peripheral vision. The unwritten rule is that if you do not acknowledge that you have seen the other vehicle, most probably you will achieve or retain the right of way. If the conflict becomes one of fender-to-fender confrontation, you can affect great surprise that the other vehicle appeared. Honking horns in this situation does not count; blinking lights, however, gives you great power.

A 1990 statistic suggested that in greater Jakarta with her 8 million people, there were over 4 million vehicles. Vigorous official campaigns aimed at driver discipline and courtesy are on-going. Amazingly, one rarely sees angry outbursts on the road. Pedestrians and villagers routinely appear as temporary traffic policemen, complete with whistles, when the traffic lights have a fainting spell or the road is impacted. Foreigners who have been here long enough to take the long view have seen the public's attitude toward disciplined driving improve. The driving public itself is less forgiving of the traffic offenders.

Chapter Three

FOREIGN TONGUES

An Old Foreign Hand who had spent most of his life working and living outside his native country gave us some good advice. Our experiences here have borne that out. Therefore, in this chapter we present some information about Bahasa Indonesia, the national language, and urge you to learn it; we explain how important the business of greeting everyone is and give you words to say that will help you get started; and we encourage you to anticipate that all news is good news here, even when it is awful! Finally, we present explanations and examples to guide you through six ways to say 'Please' and twelve ways to say 'No'.

Indonesians will immediately appreciate your efforts to speak the language. Other 'expat watchers' have noted that those foreign residents who can speak the language seem to settle in more quickly and encounter fewer of the frustrations and problems that rise to snarl at you during the day. You have much to gain and nothing to lose in speaking the language.

BAHASA INDONESIA

Most of us approach the business of speaking a new language, doing business, making requests, and being addressed in it pretty casually. The assumption is that by raising the voice, waving the arms, speaking s-l-o-w-l-y, and engaging in a bit of dramatics, almost anything can be communicated.

However, what is communicated to the Indonesians by loud voices and arms waving like semaphores is anger. Although everyone appreciates clearly articulated speech, no adult wants to be spoken to as a child. Spontaneous dramatics might be entertaining but not always effective. We are left with the fact of learning the language.

A foreign resident learns the language for the same reason the Indonesians do: to communicate. Bahasa Indonesia is understood by all but the most remote areas. Competence in the language is stated unsubtly in the local press as a 'means to pursue more knowledge and higher careers'.

The statement is clear: for the person who aspires to a better job, prestige, and social status, the key is to speak well the language of communication, education, government, and business—Bahasa Indonesia.

The Good News about Bahasa Indonesia

About 70 per cent of the national population is literate in Bahasa Indonesia. Learning Bahasa Indonesia gives the foreign resident a tool for functioning confidently, builds a bridge to the local people, and acknowledges the importance of the national language.

Fortunately, survival competence in Bahasa Indonesia is within the ability of almost everyone who lives here. It is not tonal, there is no need to learn to honk and whistle. The grammar is straightforward: there are no cases, genders, declensions or difficult conjugations. It does not contain the verb 'to be'. It is written in the familiar Roman letters.

It was and still is a language of traders—a business language—and it has no long literary history. It is basically phonetic. Since its selection as the national language in the early part of this century, Bahasa Indonesia has been correctly viewed as one of the unifiers of the country. Happily for the foreign resident, both Radio Republik Indonesia and Televisi Republik Indonesia have reinforced a common pronunciation.

Bahasa Indonesia has a large number of 'loan words' from other languages and an equally large number of Anglicised words, e.g. *konpoi* (convoy), *demokrasi* (democracy) and *opisboi* (office boy). With a little confidence born of practice, you can sail through most conversations, improvising words with elan if not accuracy!

Obviously, we suggest you supply yourself with dictionaries (see the Bibliography) and make inquiries for a teacher. It is probably helpful to get an immediate grasp on the numbers and the alphabet (so you can spell your names in Indonesian, something that is done frequently, especially when leaving telephone messages). For example, Draine and Hall would be spelt (pronounced) in Indonesian:

DRAINE	day	air	ahh	ee	enn	aae
HALL	haa	ahh	ell	ell		

Trying unsuccessfully to spell your own name can make you feel you possess a single digit IQ.

The Magic Sound of 'Yah'

Yes, Ya, Yah are words that will fall with familiar pleasure on the ears of the foreigner, especially if he is asking a question like 'Do you understand?'

The eager face smiles back, the head nods vigorously, and the magic 'Ya, ya' fall from the lips. Unfortunately, that sound does not always mean 'yes'. It most often implies the presence of life in the listener, a muscular ability to nod the head, and a driving desire to please and say whatever you want to hear. Thus ya … ya … ya.

Miscommunication, for any reason, breeds anger and frustration and promotes the tendency to label the focus of anger as stupid or ignorant.

The Function of Phonetics

Sometimes simple phonics will come to the rescue. A Chinese man in the pork market handed us a note with the following cryptic message: 'pop cap, pop lion, sperip' and a list of prices. Knowing that the letter *c* before vowels in Bahasa Indonesia is pronounced *ch* made the code comprehensible. He was acknowledging our order for pork chops, pork loin, and spareribs.

Bahasa Indonesia has its share of 'sound alike' words, e.g.

key	*kunci*	pronounced	kun chee
rabbit	*kelinci*	pronounced	klean chee
buttons	*kancing*	pronounced	kan ching
urine	*kencing*	pronounced	ken ching

The need for accuracy is obvious. We once asked the driver to get the rabbit to start the car.

There is also confusion between the word for trousers (*celana*, pronounced cha-la-na) and the word for window (*jendela*, pronounced jen-day-la). One can only imagine the agonies of the mistress of the house who informs her houseboy that he needs to wash his trousers because they are so dirty that she can't see through them!

The words *rumput* (grass) and *rambut* (hair) are also easily confused. We recall helping a friend interview a prospective cook. She was trying to describe her husband and wanted to indicate that he was 'mature' (balding). With great seriousness, she informed the cook that her husband did not have much grass on his head.

The pleasure immediately reflected in the faces of Indonesians when they hear you speak (or trying to speak) their language is an immediate return for the time spent studying. A new arrival was overheard sighing wistfully, 'My grandchildren wouldn't believe I am studying to learn my numbers.' Her grandchildren may, in fact, never appreciate that, but her household staff and the people in the stores and markets certainly will.

GREETINGS

Having just informed you of the joys and advantages of speaking Bahasa Indonesia, we hope you are ready to begin. The obvious door-opener is to learn how to greet. The formality of greeting is extremely important to Indonesians. It is more than a smile or a show of friendliness. It is an assurance of civility and a guarantee of respect. Throughout Indonesia everyone is greeted.

The most common greeting is the egalitarian salutation of Islam, '*Selamat*' (Blessings or peace). This greeting serves for high officials of government, employers and employees, your servants, the people you meet on the street, the venerably aged and the young.

One does not speak rudely or hastily to anyone. Whether you are merely leaving a note for a friend with her gardener, or inquiring about the price of tomatoes in the *pasar*, you will begin your conversation with the gentle greeting, '*Selamat*.'

This tidy greeting can be attached to a time of day or an event to suit the occasion. (See 'Indonesian Perceptions, Time ... Rubber and Otherwise'.)

The western workhorse *hello* is used in many settings here. In a restaurant, it may be used as an attention-getting word. 'Hello ... May I have some more coffee?' On the telephone, 'Hello' is usually spoken after the connecting number has been confirmed: '577-437? Hello!' The casual greeting between friends is '*Apa khabar?*' (Hey, what's the news?) and the response is '*Baik, baik sahaja, Mas*' (Everything's A-OK pal).

Throughout Asia and certainly in Indonesia the traveller may be met with 'Hello Mister!' This is directed equally at adults and children of both sexes. Acknowledge that greeting merely with a smile and do not get involved in an 'I'm not a mister, I'm a missus' sort of conversation.

In rural areas where the level of English seems to have been imbibed from television and comics, one may be greeted with, 'Hello Baby! Kiss me? Do you love me?' and similar inappropriate inquiries. Do not overreact. A gracious smile and the correct greeting, for example, '*Selamat pagi*,' offered to them will always restore order to the situation.

Words to Say

Apa khabar?	A casual inquiry between friends to ask 'What's new?' or 'How are you?' Polite but informal.
Bagaimana?	This would be roughly translated as 'How's it going?' A very casual greeting.
Selamat	The all-purpose greeting of blessings and peace. It is attached to other words as the situation requires. It is the most formal greeting word and is used with persons of all social levels.

AND THE GOOD NEWS IS ...

Having rushed out to greet the world, you may now want to employ the standard 'How are you?' questions and participate in the first level of social conversation. Here you will encounter the patina of grace; all news is good.

Avoiding Unpleasantries

No one in Indonesia wants to be the bearer of bad news. It's poor form. It's inelegant. It just isn't done. Bad or contrary news is delivered so quietly and subtly that you may not even know what is going on. The Indonesians themselves are super-sharp in this area of interpreting subtle signals while the westerner is often left feeling foolish and appearing dull.

Bad news might be couched in a list of improbable reasons why something did not happen or work or get done. Bad news may be softened with a gentle lie, delivered in a deprecating tone or with a broad smile. The formula, '*Apa khabar?*' (What's the news?) must be answered with '*Baik, baik!*' (It's all good), even if it is awful. Indonesians spend great energy and time rearranging facts to suit their need to avoid unpleasantries.

So used to speaking circuitously are the Indonesians that many are unprepared for the western tell-it-like-it-is approach to problem identification and solving. The foreigner learns to speak in circles, to approach the problem backwards, to speak in the passive voice and always to include the invisible third party in the conversation.

TALKING IN CIRCLES

Twelve Ways to Say NO

One of the ways to avoid feeling foolish when you can't hear a negation in a conversation is to learn the various expressions that imply 'No'. Demonstrating a familiarity with this information will create a sense of ease and confidence among the Indonesians that their subtleties are being understood and, as a bonus, lower your frustration level. The Indonesians go to elegant lengths to avoid speaking the word, NO. Observe:

1. *BELUM*
Not yet, nothing promised, nothing done.
Is lunch ready?
Belum. (Not yet, for unstated reasons: no food, the stove died, the cat ate the thawing chicken ...)
Are you married?
Belum. (Not yet, even though you are 85!)

2. *TIDAK USAH*
Not necessary, not required, don't worry about it.
Do you need the umbrella?
Tidak usah. (No, thank you, I don't want it.)
Did you water the plants?
Tidak usah. (No, it just rained.)

3. *LEBIH BAIK TIDAK*
This expression is used in the same situations where an English speaker would imply strong disapproval of an act by saying, 'I don't think that's such a good idea' or 'I'd rather you didn't do that.' Thus, seeing a young woman preparing to go out alone, one could say, '*Lebih baik tidak pergi luar sendiri.*' (I strongly advise you not to go out alone.)

4. *TIDAK BOLEH*
Not allowed to, not given permission
Small children will often announce, '*Tidak boleh …*' to acknowledge that they have not been given permission to do something.

5. *TIDAK SENANG*
I am not happy or contented.
In any relationship between superiors and subordinates, it is important

that the superior always feel contented with the work of the subordinate. (See 'Indonesian Perceptions, Doing Honour ... With Feeling' and 'Business, Indonesian-style, The Boss, The *Bapak*'.) Thus, if the *Nyonya* sees her houseplants dead from lack of attention, her statement, '*Saya tidak senang*' (I am very upset that you have forgotten to water them!) would be a strong expression of a negative feeling.

6. *TIDAK TERIMA*
I don't approve or give approval, cannot accept.
Tidak terima is used in the same situations where English speakers would say, 'You've got to be putting me on!' or 'Do I need this?' or 'I refuse to believe that!' or 'Give me a break!' It states a rejection of the information or opinion being offered.

7. *JANGAN*
Don't! An exclamation to avert disaster, implies retribution, consequences, as in '*Jangan duduk di sini.*' (Don't sit here.)

8. *BUKAN*
This is often drawn out when spoken, as in *Buuukan!*
Who did this?
Bukan saya! (Not me!)

9. *ENGGAK*
A guttural, unattractive sound suggesting you are trying to remove a cockroach from your throat. It is Jakarta slang for '*tidak*'.

10. *TIDAK*
This is rarely used alone. It is usually attached to the verb '... want to' (*mahu*) and implies that you 'don't want to ...'.
Do you want to eat?
Tidak mahu. (No, thank you.)

11. *TERIMA KASIH*

Thank you. But, if delivered with a vague smile and a light shake of the head, it means 'No, thank you.'

Would you like tea?

Terima kasih. (No, thank you.)

(You would accept the arrival of tea with a brief nod. In polite situations you would not ask for a drink; it would simply arrive. If the need supercedes politeness, e.g. a thirsty child, then instead of asking for a drink, you state the problem: '*Dia haus.*' He is thirsty.)

12. *MA'AF TIDAK*

A very strong but polite 'No, I'm sorry. I don't want to ...'

Would you donate money, madam?

Ma'af tidak! (No, I'm sorry, I will not.)

Actually, there is another way that 'No' is expressed. When the Indonesian is speaking in English and you hear 'Yes, but ...,' you are hearing 'No.' The negation follows the word 'but'.

Six Ways to Say PLEASE

There is absolutely nothing vague about saying 'please'. Indonesians make very fine distinction between asking for physical assistance, begging, requesting—shades of meaning, all usually embraced by 'please ...' in English. A working knowledge of this information will endear you to your household and office staff.

1. *TOLONG*

Implies a request for physical assistance. An English equivalent would be 'Here, give me a hand.'

Tolong cuci piring. (Please wash the dishes.)

In the traditional sense, the use of *tolong* indicates the shared assumption of a burden. *Minta tolong dari Tuan dan Nyonya untuk bikin rumah.* (Please give us money to build a house.)

2. *MINTA*

Request, ask that something be done.

Minta beli jeruk di pasar. (Please buy some oranges in the *pasar*.)

3. *CUBA*

Try, attempt.

Cuba buka botol ini. (Please open this bottle.)

4. *HARAP*

Hope, expect.

Saya harap anda bisa datang. (Please come. We hope you will come.)

5. *SILAKAN*

This is a very formal formula word for 'please ...' (... eat, be seated, begin, etc.).

Silakan minum. (Please enjoy your drink.)

6. *MOHON*

Beseech, beg. It is a word of supplication.

Mohon ma'afkan saya datang terlambat. (Please excuse me for coming late.)

THE JAVANESE ALPHABET

Of all the aspects of Javanese culture, probably their alphabet best illustrates the profound cultural ties with the Hindus. Their script, Devanagri, is obviously the source for the orthographical signs of Javanese. A glimpse at the Javanese script will immediately evoke gratitude that Bahasa Indonesia with its Roman characters was chosen to be the common language.

Javanese is the vehicle of Javanese literature and much of the history of Indonesia. Many are literate in it. One of the most charming tales about the language is the method used to teach the alphabet.

The sounds of the letters tell a little story. We illustrate the tale with Javanese script, the modern English syllable sounds, and the tale as recorded by Sir Stamford Raffles, who was a fan of Java and the Javanese.

ha na ca ra ka

There were two warriors . . .

da ta sa wa la

disputing with each other . . .

pa da ja ya nya

equally courageous . . .

ma ga ba ta nga

till they both died.

Chapter Four

FOOD, WONDERFUL FOOD!

This chapter discusses the variety of foods in Indonesia. We introduce you to some of them and encourage you to realise how they are a focus for national identity and pride. We discuss some comparisons between food values and eating styles East and West and point out the taboos that lurk in the murk of the ethnic mix here.

THE MOVABLE FEAST

Indonesia is truly a feast: whether in eating styles, charm, price or ambience, there is something for everyone. One of the first memories that the expatriate will have in Indonesia is that the food comes to you. It is pushed through the windows of cars at traffic intersections, hustled at the bus-stops, hastily sold as trains pause at stations.

These little bundles of food are commonly called *bungkusan* (something wrapped in a banana leaf or paper). Usually they are bundles of rice and condiments in banana leaves, skewered shut with a small sharp stick or palm leaf rib and steamed. The banana leaf serves as cooking vessel, carry-out container, and finally the plate. Thrown on the ground, the banana leaf quickly biodegrades into vegetable humus. Lately, however, more and more foods are being wrapped in plastic. These discarded wrappings clutter the rivers and canals and create unsightly messes along the roads, causing general environmental concern.

The *rantang*, the ultimate lunchbox, is a series of containers stacked and held together by a long handle. They can contain rice, meat, fish, soup, fruit … an entire meal. People carry these from home. Energetic entrepreneurs have also developed a business of providing lunches to office workers. Late in the morning the *rantang* person will appear in the office elevator or stairwells with arm-loads of the containers to be delivered to the employees' desks. It is quite common to see lower-level office and shop workers eating at their desks or, more probably, seated on the floor in a group.

One friend told of her experience at one of the large embassies in Jakarta. Arriving for a lunch date, she appeared at the security window to present her credentials. It seemed no one was in the office. She made little 'hello' noises and rapped on the glass. The secretary appeared from under her desk where she had been sitting on the floor eating her lunch from its banana leaf wrapping.

Street Food Vendors

The traditional convenience foods in Indonesia are those served by the colourful *kaki lima* men. They provide the material for memories of many of the sights and sounds of life in Indonesia. These men push their carts in every town and *kampung*, passing along local news and gossip as well as providing cheap food.

Early in the morning you will hear the whistle of the *bubur ayam* man selling his breakfast dish of chicken porridge. As the day wears on, he is followed by the *Teng! Teng!* of the *cendol* man beating a spoon on the edge of a glass that he would like to fill with shredded fruit, pudding, and sweet syrup for you. *Tok! Tok!* is the sound of the *bakso* man beating on a small wooden gong. He will fill your

The kaki lima men and carts are a familiar sight in villages and towns

Entire meals are served up from this 'shoulder-pole' kitchen.

bowl with the soup and *bakso*, small balls of pounded meat, chicken, or fish. The high-pitched *Ting! Ting!* of a spoon tapped rhythmically on the edge of one of the typical 'rooster' soup bowls tells you the *bakmi* man, the noodle seller, is at the gate. At night, children listen for the high, sustained whistle of the *putu* man's steamer. He sells a divine confection of steamed rice flour, tapioca, melted brown sugar and shredded coconut. The sharp *Tay! Tay!* of the *saté* man carries clearly in the night air to remind you that he will grill wonderful shreds of seasoned meats as you wait.

Caution: Most of the foods sold by the *kaki lima* men are freshly prepared. You might make two significant observations: first that all the bowls provided by the *kaki lima* man are rinsed in a bucket of water which hangs from his wagon, and second, that almost all the housewives and servants who buy from the *kaki lima* men take their own dishes to be filled.

Night Food Stalls

Special foods are sold from permanent night stalls. The 'street foods' are rarely cooked in the home. This is where you find *martabak*, a meat-and-egg omelette which is almost a meal.

Warungs, small neighbourhood eateries that seat 4–6 around a table, are always visible. Some specialise in coffee and bottled drinks, others have soups and rice dishes that are usually cooked in the home of the owner and then brought to the *warung* to be sold.

The Rumah Makan

The *rumah makan* is the complete restaurant. Foods can be cooked to order in the kitchen. They will also wrap to carry out and there is usually a broad selection of pre-cooked foods which can be purchased, or warmed up (for the westerner).

In some of the *rumah makan* you might discover that the menu has more pages than the local newspaper. Don't overreact. The six or eight pages of food choices don't always reflect what is actually

55

available. It might only indicate they could probably cook all those things, or that they wish they could, or that they feel such a list is expected of them! Rather than endure a shower of '*Ma'af, tidak ada*' or '*Sudah habis*' (Sorry, not available ... Supply exhausted!) from the waiter, it is better and certainly less frustrating to inquire what they have that is ready and fresh: '*Sedia makanan apa?*'

Fast Food Restaurants

It used to be that the only fast food eateries in town were those that guaranteed a speedy case of diarrhoea. Now throughout the islands there is a wide variety of western fast food chains selling chicken grilled, roasted, steamed and fried, pizza, American hamburgers and donuts, and ice cream. Japanese fast food establishments and Korean barbeques round out the recent ethnic food scene. These places are usually filled with Indonesian families and a healthy number of expatriates queued up for 'a taste of home'.

One of the interesting effects of the plastic restaurants is a heavy emphasis on cleanliness and quick service. This is in contrast with the 'good old days' when foreigners would swap tales of cats and rats at the fish restaurants along the harbours, of dogs which line up for scraps everywhere in Bali, and the restaurant rodents who gained a certain notoriety for their predictable appearances and performances in a number of well known restaurants.

International Quality Restaurants

One sees in the larger cities more international quality restaurants usually filled with appreciative patrons. Some of these have well deserved fine reputations and almost all have high prices!

FOOD, THE ETHNIC IDENTIFIER

Young Indonesian professionals were asked what their major concern would be if they were suddenly transferred from Jakarta. It was expected that the answers would reflect the feeling of separation from the extended family, or being unsure of how to make new friends, or a sense of distance from their ethnic group. Wrong! Wrong! Without exception, they expressed a concern that the food might be different from what they were used to.

Indonesians identify closely with their ethnic foods and like to see foreigners enjoying them. The foreigner feels the same sort of pleasure combined with a sense of personal acceptance when he is complimented on his food. Like me—like my food.

While some foods, such as *nasi goreng* (fried rice), can be considered broadly Indonesian, many serve as provincial identifiers. And just as Holland has the Gouda cheese, France the quiche Lorraine, England the Lancashire hot pot, and America the Georgia peach, so does Indonesia label certain foods by area.

Nasi liwet (white rice and chicken in coconut cream) is always associated with Solo in Central Java. Anyone who confesses a fondness for *nasi jaha* and *onde-onde* is a fan of Minahasa cooking. *Sayur assam* (sour vegetables) is from West Java but *sayur lodeh* (mixed vegetables in coconut cream) is from Central Java. Any food from a *rumah makan* Padang is guaranteed to do for your sinuses what the doctors have failed to do! It is said that when you eat Padang food, the next thing you do—whether you scream, swallow, spit it out, or weep as your lips char—is wrong! If you are a real fan, you gasp, 'Oh, wonderful,' as the blisters form on your lips, and nod vigorously (because you can't speak) as your eyes and nose run in moist assent that this is truly grand! truly grand!

Indeed, the variety and quality of the cooked food is considered a national asset. One prominent promoter of Indonesian cuisine at all levels is Mr Joop Ave. In his previous capacity as Chief of Protocol, he gave a dinner for Her Majesty Queen Elizabeth in London, presenting a wide variety of Indonesian foods. In his current position as Director General of Tourism, Mr Ave has asserted that the delicious foods of the various regions should attract tourists, citing the fiery Padang (West Sumatra) cooking, the *pepeda* of the

Moluccas, and the dishes from Menado (Sulawesi), Sunda (West Java), and Central Java.

Indonesia's cuisine, in both ingredients and preparation, reflects the various tastes of the Chinese, Indian, Arab, Dutch, and Portuguese people who have lived in the archipelago through the centuries. Given this mix, how could the foods not be tasty?

One of the greatest appeals of Indonesian cooking is the principle of contrast; for each spicy dish there is one to cool the palate. In practice this principle of culinary counterpoint lends itself to an exercise in enjoyable excess with a multitude of courses serving as a showcase for the variety of foods. Presenting tables groaning with food, sumptuous feasts are the norm. The most familiar of these marathon meals is the *rijstaffel* (rice table), traditionally served by lines of servants, each offering a different selection.

The nation's favourite fruits are usually advertised by area, for example, *jeruk* Bali (a large pomelo-type grapefruit), *salak* Bali (a marvellous lizard-skinned fruit), the exceptional mangoes from Probollingo, East Java, the *jeruk* Garut (sweet tangerines from the Puncak area south of Jakarta, or the *duku* (sweet lychee-like fruit) from Palembang in Sumatra. Your ability to match fruit to area delights Indonesians and provides pleasant, casual conversation.

UNUSUAL AND UNEXPECTED FOODS

Widely throughout Asia and certainly in Indonesia, almost every part of the animal appears on the menu. An Indonesian friend told us that when he was a student in Australia his wife wanted to cook some of his favourite food, which required the use of offal. They told the butcher that the offal was for the dog. They were probably being very wise. Yet, if anyone had sampled the delicious food his wife prepared, the price of offal would have increased considerably!

Here are some of the more unusual dishes you will see on the menu of an Indonesian *warung* or *rumah makan*.

Belut blado **(eel):** This dish with copious amounts of chilli sauce comes from the Minangkabau of West Sumatra.

Dog: The Batak of North Sumatra and the Minahasa of northern Sulawesi find dog, especially black dog, tasty. Everyone knows this bit of doggerel:
> The mouse is afraid of the cat,
>> The cat is afraid of the dog,
>>> The dog is afraid of the Minahasa!

Gulai kambing **(goat curry):** Any dish with the name *gulai* has the distinctive blend of spices which make up Indonesian curry.

Gulai otak **(beef brain curry):** This is a very hot spicy curry from the Minangkabau of West Sumatra.

Jeroan goreng: This is a fried intestine dish using the lungs, liver, chicken giblets and kidneys. It originated on Java but is now considered pan-Indonesian.

'How about a peanut butter and jelly sandwich?'

Pecel lele (**catfish**): Catfish chopped and cooked with *kemangi* (herbal, similar to lime) leaves and chilli sauce. It has an extremely strong smell.

Sambal goreng saren (**fried dried chicken's blood**): This very nutritious food is often given to children.

Sop kaki kambing (**leg of goat soup**): This has goat sinew, mixed with intestines, chopped penis, lungs and bladder, all blended together in coconut cream.

Soto (**soup from Madura**): This has vegetables, meat and intestines.

Soto ayam: Indonesia's entry in the international chicken soup contest and most of us would rank it Number One! It is a wonderful light broth flavoured with lemon grass and other herbs and spices to which the diner adds his choice of glass noodles, sliced hardboiled eggs, shredded chicken, chopped shallots, fried potatoes, beansprouts, *emping* (crackers), fresh lime juice and *sambal* (chilli sauce). Divine!

Usus gajah (**literally, elephant's intestines**): Perhaps once upon a time this was a dish for kings using ingredients from elephants, but today beef is used. This fried dish is usually topped with an egg.

Definitely different and usually very sweet are some of the lumpy drinks like *es cendol* and *es adpokat* and the coconut milk based drinks which often have sugar syrup and large pieces of coconut added to them.

SPECIAL BELIEFS ABOUT FOOD
While rice is widely regarded as a symbol of sustenance and bounty, it produces one interesting negative effect. Many young children have rotting and pitted front teeth because of a childhood eating

habit: they hold the rice under their upper lip and against their teeth. The natural sugar of rice attacks dental enamel. Adult teeth are usually strong and without decay.

Ubi (white or yellow sweet potato) is considered 'poor man's food' and thus might not be the best choice to serve to discriminating Indonesian guests. The exception would be if you are serving baked turkey or ham and candied sweet potatoes (*ubi kuning*). You may explain that this is a western traditional meal and your Indonesian guests will not be offended. They might just tell you that candied sweet potatoes are called *kolak* here and are often served as a teatime snack.

While almost everyone will eat boiled or steamed vegetables, only the Sundanese of West Java eat raw vegetables (*lalap*). This may explain why some of your Indonesian guests avoid the vegetable dip and the tossed salad.

Javanese women generally avoid eating fish when they are nursing. Certainly on Java—according to our sources, throughout the islands—many women will try to avoid eating cucumber, pineapple and banana as these are thought to make the vaginal membranes too moist.

Not only Muslims, but also some members of other religions avoid eating pork. Some cooks will even refuse to touch it in the kitchen. Most Muslims would appreciate being told if pork is being served. If it is, it should be on a separate table from the general buffet and never on the same plate with other foods.

Most Indonesians observe the dietary restrictions that exist for them in their ethnic or religious groups. However, almost every expatriate has encountered exceptions to some of the traditional food taboos. It is helpful to acknowledge and accept them as a measure of the differences between individuals.

Chapter Five

INDONESIAN PERCEPTIONS

Perceptions: way of seeing. How many phrases are there to express that idea? Point of view ... world view ... personal perspective ... personal values ... reason for being. They all suggest that the process of making sense of what we see around us is heavily weighted in each individual's way of looking at the situation.

The villager who shifts to the city finds the values that worked in the fields and *desa* (small villages) do not fit in the city. He is isolated, exposed, away from the security of the family and the comfort of the group's concern. The rhythm of working cooperatively in the fields has given way to a frantic hustle for day wages.

Not only do we find points of view and values shifting with the situation and with the individual, they shift among representatives of different ethnic groups.

An anecdote is often cited to explain the differing reactions of various Indonesian *suku* (ethnic groups) to the same situation. A man had his toe trod upon. If he were Batak, he would scowl savagely and immediately vent his displeasure in loud, direct, abusive terms ... and do nothing; if Javanese, he would clear his throat politely, gesture vaguely in the direction of the offended digit, call a large group around him and arrive at a decision by consensus to possibly do something about it sometime; if he were Balinese, he would pray; if he were Bugis or Madurese, he would immediately beat up the person; if he were Padang, he would offer some money to make it all right.

This much loved anecdote allows a perspective of 360 degrees and acknowledges that most of us spend a lot of time clinging to and being hampered (sometimes) by our point of view.

And when ethnic and national business and social values meet and mix ... well, that is what the rest of the book is all about.

BARGAINING

Depending on your point of view, the business of bargaining can be: a method of solidifying your position in the local economic community; a pleasant pastime; a technique for saving money; a vexatious frustration; an expected courtesy; a social vehicle for requesting and receiving favours; an example of unevolved and unsophisticated economics.

Judge gently! Throughout Asia for many, bargaining over the price of goods and services is an art form as complicated as a dance, as expressive as a fine painting or poem, as affirming as the practice of religion. Bargaining as understood by the practitioners is definitely a method for establishing and solidifying one's status in the economic community—an item may have a variety of prices, each reflecting in the eye of the merchant the correct price for each of his customers. To offer everyone the same price removes the opportunity to 'do a favour for my special customer' and equally the opportunity to blatantly overcharge an unsuspecting buyer!

Few are those in Asia who do not smile when a preferred price is offered to them as a 'courtesy' (for being a *langganan*, a customer). Equally flattering is it to be the recipient of an extra fruit, an extra spray of flowers, an additional potted plant as a favour, a small gift.

As one bargains and prices are bandied back and forth, there is ample time to ask about the progress of the children, or share some local gossip. Of course one must feel a sense of conquest at the amount of money saved, but most people would admit this is not the real purpose of bargaining.

The typical westerner-in-a-hurry is confused and vexed at the resistance to doing business quickly. Many foreigners will spend much time looking for the 'fixed price' stores and embrace the goods and services there like familiar friends.

'Unevolved and lacking sophistication' is the general snarl of the westerner who looks limply about for the familiar green screen of the checkout computerised cash register and only encounters a smiling *tukang* digging in twelve pockets for the bits of change.

How the System Works

In the larger cities of Indonesia, many of the stores are now 'fixed price'—predictable, efficient, impersonal and standardised. However, in the smaller shops bargaining or at least asking for discounts is the rule. When in doubt, smile and ask for a discount, round off the bill to an even amount a bit lower than the total. What can you lose?

In the street stalls that sell merchandise (not food), bargaining is usually the rule. Start at about 50–60 per cent of the first price and raise your offer a bit as the first price is lowered until an agreement is reached (which should be 10–12 per cent lower than the original). This may take 15–30 minutes as you take time to comment on everyone else's purchases, remark on the weather and make general small talk while the prices are being considered. Do not hesitate to shrug your shoulders and walk away. The chances are excellent that you will be followed and the deal set.

It is important to realise that if the *tukang* agrees to your price or you to his, you are obliged to purchase. It is extremely poor form to agree to a price and not agree to buy. It is also poor form to make bargaining a personal issue or to become angry. Bargaining is a pastime, a social encounter played back and forth like a game. Also remember that the *tukangs* have memories like traps and will file for future reference everything about the sale.

Many expatriates have reported that they get so used to bargaining and so comfortable with the system that they continue to bargain in their home countries … often with success.

Words to Say

Bagaimana	What do you think (of my offer)?
Berapa rupiah, ini? (*Ini berapa?*)	How much is this?
Harganya berapa?	What's the price?
Laris!	Sold! Probably, you will see the *tukang* slap his goods with the money as he utters the word, *laris*, wishing the remaining goods to be desirable, and sought after.
Masa!	Impossible! How can that be? Best said with hand on heart as you prepare to faint in response to being asked a ridiculously high price.
Rugi!	Loss! Usually moaned by the *tukang* in response to your fainting spell and gasps of '*Masa, masa.*'
Untung!	Good luck! A bonus! Usually uttered by you as you depart with your purchase and by the *tukang* as he tucks away your money.

BATHING

Every Indonesian would appreciate the remark of the foreigner who sighed that her favourite memory of Indonesia was the sound of bath water splashing in the *mandi* throughout the day. Indeed, not only is it a happy sound to hear, it describes an extremely important activity for all Indonesians.

Being clean and bathing frequently—a minimum of twice a day for most—is a significant Indonesian characteristic. The joy of cleanliness is a topic for general conversation. Everyone has heard young Indonesian children announce exultantly, '*Sudah mandi!*' (I've just bathed!) A polite question asked by visitors in Central Java about 4 p.m. is, 'How are you? Have you had your bath yet?' If the response is 'No' it is perfectly correct to hasten to the bath while the visitor waits.

Wet is Clean (running water is very clean!)

Bathing Indonesian splash-style is an energetic activity. Water is flung about the entire area—floor, walls, and sometimes ceiling — to the exclamations of joy or anguish at its temperature. (Heated water is for the ill, the very young, or the foreigner.) The western tendency to install deep pile carpets in bathrooms is viewed with alarm by some Indonesians for whom much of the pleasure of bathing is the absolute unrestrained wetness of it!

The *tempat mandi* (bathing place) may be a western bathroom, a small room in the rear of the house, an outdoor space enclosed by a woven mat, or in rural situations, a handy spot on the river bank.

It is possible that a bathing area will be shared by several families. The towel, soap, shampoo are carried to and from the bath site. Generally, people bathe standing in rubber sandals, because the floor might be cement or tile, but it could also be sand, boards, stone or hard-packed earth. Indonesians snort at the true tales of westerners who climbed into the *bak mandi* and thought it very uncomfortable. The *bak* is a container for bathing water, not a bathtub.

Bathing Native Style ...

... is not always in the nude. If you are bathing in a walled, roofed room, strip and splash! In a village, at the riverside, or in a small enclosure with only a woven-mat wall, women should bathe in a *sarung* wrapped from the armpits down. When you finish, wrap a dry *sarung* around you, hold the ends of it loosely in your teeth or in one hand, then unwrap and drop the wet *sarung*. The dry one now becomes a towel/garment. Men bathing in an exposed setting should wear shorts. Children under the age of 8 or so can frolic about nude without offending anyone.

Running Water Isn't Music to All!

It is the responsibility of each bather to leave the area clean and the water containers full. In the villages, most Indonesians will cheerfully turn on the water and then walk away, secure in the knowledge that someone will hear the sound of overflowing water and come to turn it off. This tendency is carried into urban business and domestic settings ... in the driveway, bathroom or kitchen.

Foreigners quite understandably leap to the conclusion that there is a major plumbing problem because of the wetness of the walls and floors of bathrooms in offices and public buildings. Men are often seen emerging from them with trousers rolled up to the knees, which to the western mind indicates FLOOD! The tendency to leave the water running and to flush not only the toilet but also the walls and the toilet seat creates great frustration for the foreigner who is conditioned to turn water off.

Mosquito Breeding in the Bak Mandi

In the past, people used to keep goldfish and other small fish in the *bak mandi* to prevent the breeding of mosquitoes, a carrier of dengue haemorrhagic fever. Now this is only commonly done in the villages. Chemicals for use in the *bak mandi* to control mosquito breeding are available at the local health centres, and the public is being educated about this.

The Business of Bathrooming

Expatriates tend to panic at the lack of pedestal toilets that flush inside rooms with doors that lock. Searching for those facilities, often in vain, they sometimes expect heroism from their bladders and bowels. However, in Indonesia no one has any false modesty about bodily needs. The important thing is to attend to them in a timely and rational fashion. Villagers in many areas will walk great distances to defecate in the river (*kali*), or dig a small hole and then cover it. What is not acceptable is to leave a mess for someone else to discover or clean.

Caution: As tidy as the behaviour described above is, do remember that the streams and rivers, bathing pools of many areas, are obviously and unavoidably home to most of the waterborne intestinal parasites common in tropical Asia. The apparently clear water is often full of organisms that would make it possible for you to read *War and Peace* at one sitting in the bathroom.

In the villages, when one asks either to bathe or to go to the bathroom, he must be certain to give very clear requests. (See 'Words to Say', page 71.)

While it is a common practice to urinate at the bathing site, one does not have a bowel movement there. It is expected that you will make that request clear (you may be asked!) and you will be shown to a pit or a ditch maintained by the family for that purpose. Usually, but not always, those pits are 'flushed' with water or a scoopful of dirt. A glance around should indicate the correct practice at the place.

It is now increasingly common to see the *bak mandi* (for bathing) and the squat toilet (W.C.) sharing the same room in almost all the restaurants, train stations, airports, bus-stops throughout Indonesia. The water from the *bak mandi* is dippered out to flush the toilet and also meant to be used by anyone who wants a quick and refreshing bath. This is a boon for travellers in Indonesia.

The Squat Toilet

Westerners who are unfamiliar with squat toilets generally view them with alarm. The fact remains that they are used by well over half the world's people.

In Indonesia, for convenience, people usually remove their underwear or trousers to a hook or nail. There are several reasons for this. The first is that it is more comfortable to have your knees free and not in a death grip with your garments. The second is that the contents of your pockets are protected from a precipitous and unplanned trip into the toilet. (Retrieving these goods may not be an experience you would want to write home about!) The third reason is, having protected your clothes from unplanned precipitation, you will want to keep them high and dry during the splash of the flushing. Once you have tried to pour water delicately into only the hole of the squat toilet, you will discover why one flings with force and abandon and flushes the entire area.

Don't look for a roll of toilet paper in the traditional W.C.'s. Brief children well on this topic or do the obvious: carry your own roll. The operative word is wash, not wipe. Commonly, the left hand and copious amounts of water are used to complete the bathroom chores. Remember, the left hand is used exclusively for this procedure and now you know why you would never handle goods or food or eat with your left hand!

There are very few bathroom taboos for young children. Wet pants and other moist mistakes are viewed calmly by parents. Children's clothes are changed and the offending puddles mopped up without fuss.

Bathroom habits that are acceptable in the villages do not always make the shift to trains, aeroplanes and big city ceramic facilities. Persons on aeroplanes for the first time are given instructions about using chemical toilets. It is common to see anguished attendants in the bathrooms of major airports, watching and instructing villagers whose inclination (for comfort and cleanliness) is to climb on top of the toilet seat.

Bathroom Fragrances

The most commonly encountered air freshener in bathrooms is a pile of mothballs. This is not to imply that Indonesia has a super moth which attacks ceramics. Rather the camphor balls serve to keep cockroaches at bay, inhibit the growth of fungus, and at least change the air if not freshen it. In areas where water pressure is low, the compensation for cleanliness seems to be mountains of mothballs.

Do/Taboo
- Pursue your cleaning chores with confidence even if you draw a crowd. A bit of clowning with a toothbrush, comb or shampoo will ease the tension and win friends.
- Leave the area clean.
- Plan to carry your own toilet paper and towelettes with you.

- Thank whoever gave you assistance. *Menumpang mandi* (borrowing the bathing facilities) is a long-recognised part of Indonesian hospitality.
- Do not bathe in the nude in public. Be discreet.
- The bathing site should not be confused with the area for other bathroom activities.

Vocabulary

Bak mandi	The cement or tiled container that holds the bath water in the bathing area.
Gayung	Dipper—it may be a small tin can or a plastic bucket.
Kamar mandi	Bathing room or area.
W.C.	Toilet. This is pronounced 'way say'. It is not the bath area!
Mandi	To bathe, or a bath.

Words to Say

Permisi, boleh menumpang mandi?	Excuse me, may I have a bath?
Ada W.C.?	Is there a toilet? It is implied that you want to use it. Be prepared for the next bit of dialogue.
Mahu buang air kecil.	I need to urinate. You may be shown to what looks like the bathing area.
Mahu buang air besar.	I need to have a bowel movement. You will probably be shown a pit or a trench in a village or a squat toilet in an urban dwelling.

71

BEING A CHEERFUL GIVER

One notices immediately throughout Indonesia the graceful use of hands. Here, we are speaking about hands bearing gifts. Indonesians love to give presents. In a sense, it is part of the national ethic. It reinforces the sense of sharing in their communal life. The foreign resident may be included in some of these moments; at the least, it is helpful to know what some of the common 'giving' situations are.

1. When the *Tuan* or *Nyonya* returns from a long trip, the domestic staff would appreciate *ole-ole*, a small gift in the manner of a souvenir.

2. When anyone travels to an area recognised for food specialties, it is appropriate to bring some back for all: *salak* fruit from Bali, *gula Jawa* from Central Java, or even fish from a trip to the beach.

3. A gift of food is often given to express gratitude for services rendered.

4. In most ethnic groups, the dividing up of food and sharing it with guests to take home at the end of a party is common. (This is generosity mixed with common sense. Not everyone has refrigeration capacity to store large amounts of party leftovers.)

5. When a guest, especially for a meal, in the home of an Indonesian, it is usual to give a small gift to the hostess. A tin of cookies, candy, a bunch of flowers—any of these could be given to the hostess with no special ceremony.

6. When official groups (office workers, schoolchildren, social groups, etc.) visit factory sites or whatever, it is customary to present *kenang-kenangan* (mementos) of the occasion. Between Indonesians, these are usually little flags on standards or engraved plates and stands. Some foreigners keep a stock of picture books about their country on hand for this occasion.

7. *Hadiah* is a prize. There will be a *hadiah* of a drinking glass in a bucket of soap powder or a *hadiah* offered to the winner in contests.

8. *Kado* is the name for a gift given in response to an invitation (to a birthday, wedding, etc.). Thus wrapping paper is called *kertas kado* and special occasion cards are called *kartu kado*.

While the tendency to give something away in response to a compliment is not as strong here as it is in other parts of Asia, do be aware that if you gush greatly over something, you may be taking it home with you! Be genuine but moderate in your enthusiasm until you learn how to read the signals correctly.

Do/Taboo

- Be aware that formal thanks are not expected or given here as they are in the West.
- Be reassured that your Indonesian friends will remember what you give, and may refer to it much later. Many Indonesians keep lists of what people have done for them and given them, so that when the moment is right, the pay-back or reimbursement can be equal to or better than what was originally given.
- Gifts will not be opened when they are given. That is usually done later in the privacy of the immediate family. There are exceptions. Many expatriates report that when they have received gifts after making a speech or some presentation, people eagerly wait for the gift to be opened. Look for signals in the group that will guide you to do the correct and pleasing thing.

FURRED, FEATHERED, AND FINNED

It is said that Prophet Muhammed cut a space around his prayer rug rather than disturb a cat sleeping on it. This is probably why Indonesians give cats special regard.

Foreigners immediately note the cats with wrinkled, stubby or bent tails (a genetic flaw). They are found all over the islands, but Java is home to most. They are small, prefer to eat rice and fish, are found in garbage piles, *pasars* and on the roofs of houses where they chase rats in their capacity of 'turf-guarder'. Some cats will hunt rats and other vermin, but most domestic ones prefer to hunt for the maid to feed them.

Local dogs (*anjing kampung*) look like feral dogs the world over, are clever, durable and territorial. There is no history of problems with dogs running in packs. Dogs may not be shipped to Bali because of the threat of disease to the huge population of Balinese dogs. Expatriates routinely ship dogs to other postings in Indonesia or buy them from kennels. Rabies is present but not a serious threat to domestic, well cared for animals.

Indonesians, like many other Asians, are bird fanciers. Because of the mild weather, cages are usually hung outside in trees or run up on long poles. Singing birds are adored, expensive, and their owners envied; cassette tapes of champion songbirds are usually sold in the stores. Taman Mini Indonesia Indah (Beautiful Indonesia in Miniature) near Jakarta has a lovely walk-in bird enclosure where many of the birds can be seen in their natural settings.

There are snakes here, but mostly in the outer areas of a town. Few are kept as pets. Every now and then there is mention of a whopper of a python that has been caught, usually in East Java. The poisonous snakes are normally shy.

Do/Taboo

- Be aware that your dogs and cats probably eat more regularly and ingest more protein than the people who live in the *kampungs* around you.
- Be assured that many Indonesians are very sensitive to the feelings of foreigners whose beloved pet dies. Servants have been known to wrap the animals in shrouds for burial, to sprinkle them with scented water, to cover them with flower petals or to have a *selamatan* to ease the grief of the owner.
- Muslim household staff may not want to pet, play with, or walk the dog.

DOING HONOUR ... WITH FEELING

It is widely felt that the highly refined social behaviour of the Javanese more or less sets the social standards throughout the country. The expatriate arriving in Indonesia is immediately aware of this.

This behaviour either fascinates or frustrates the westerner trying to interact with it. An intellectual analysis suggests that this restraint is the product of centuries of the Hindu influence, and there are libraries of books commenting on and refining all this history. But it still does not explain why your driver laughs when he tells you that his infant son just died.

The Javanese acknowledge that they mask their emotions and rarely reveal how they feel. 'It's hard to get to know us,' they challenge. 'Once you do, we are good friends,' they promise.

The rice farmer who can't speak precisely about mystical under-pinnings and sophisticated behaviour knows that everyone has his place, that there is security in being calm and having a soul at peace. Somewhere in all this is the foreigner, trying hard to do the right thing. Whether one's rationale is cosmic, traditional, or just good manners, begin by understanding that:

1. Everyone has status in Indonesia.
2. No one is equal.
3. Status is situational.
4. There's no such thing as 'No respect'.
5. The concepts of *malu* (social shame), *gengsi* (appearances), *asal bapak senang* (keep the boss happy) and *memojokan* (being put in a corner) direct most social and many official interactions.

Everyone has Status

We recall arriving one late afternoon in a three-building village in an isolated section of West Java. Dirty from travelling, we nevertheless disembarked from our muddied Land Rovers to greet, with proper ceremony, the headman of the village and his wife, from whom we hoped to receive shelter for the night. That her teeth

75

were only a memory and his working hours were spent behind a caribou did not alter the fact that, right then, we were honour givers!

This became obvious as another group of travellers arrived, equally muddy, and equally in need of room and bathing privileges. They did not observe the formalities of greeting. Instead, they demanded service and accommodation. In a gentle, implacable Javanese way, the old woman indicated that she could not assist them. She confided to us later, 'My feelings were hurt. They didn't honour (greet) my husband with the respect his position deserved.'

No One is Equal

Indonesians go to great lengths to 'do honour' (pay respect). A diplomat recounted a scene where provincial Indonesian officials were hosting diplomatic visitors of approximately the same status. There was much 'You first ...' 'No, you ...' 'Please ...' 'After you ...' as all tried to pass through doors and get seated. Then a further pause as the group checked for visual clues to try to pass/assume/ avoid the responsibility for beginning the meeting.

Status is Situational

One does honour by forgiving tardiness, inconveniences, interruptions caused to you by a person of higher status. You are expected to be calm and understanding (on the surface at least). Not to be so would be lacking good manners, *kurang ajar*. However, your turn comes because your household staff is expected to cheerfully warm up dinner if you arrive late and unannounced. Status and its responsibilities shift with the situation and the persons involved.

Let us examine some of the typical 'showing respect' situations the expatriate is likely to encounter.

There's No Such Thing as 'No Respect'

One does honour by arriving at a function early to wait for the honoured guest. The concept of 'Hurry up and wait' was not invented

A maid honours the guest by having her head lower than his and placing left hand lightly on right upper arm.

here. It is, however, practised a lot. One does honour by escorting a guest to his car; by shaking hands with everyone as one enters and leaves a social function; by not discussing unpleasant items. One shows respect to the elderly of all social levels.

A host does honour by leaving guests in the sitting room while he changes, makes tea, and sets out the cookies. Then both host and guest are prepared to observe the civilities. No one mentions the unattended wait.

One does honour by shielding someone from bad news. If that fails, one should impart bad news with a smile! It is this situation particularly that has caused some expatriate residents to feel they are losing sanity. Reports of dying children, loss of home and land, dreadful personal tragedy are often delivered with a deprecating giggle or sustained laugh. Nobody truly thinks it is funny. The proper response would be murmurings of concern.

The outward show of civility is more important than an encounter with the truth of the situation. Thus food and drink must be offered to guests, even if the cookies are stale. Not to offer what you have is worse than offering fatigued cookies. Everyone would understand the gracious gesture. This also applies to interpersonal relationships. A super-bright office worker would always defer to a dull and plodding supervisor because of the difference in status.

Malu

The condition of *malu* is rendered loosely as loss of face or embarrassment. Stated more bluntly, to make someone *malu* is to strip the façade of status from him and expose his human imperfection. Thus, it is possible to 'do honour' by permitting someone to make a fool of himself, rather than risk the embarrassment of calling it to his attention.

Servants use the term *malu* frequently to explain away shy behaviour in their children. *Malu* is often used to excuse the avoidance of confrontation with authority.

Malu can imply a sense of deep shame for any number of reasons. Servants' minor (or major) transgressions, usually heavily coloured with a desire not to confront an unpleasant situation, can cause extreme *malu* for the individual. Many have been known to leave their employment unannounced to avoid a confrontation.

Individuals are not chastised publicly. That would allow others to witness his shame, and not allow him to describe it in his own (perhaps altered) terms. A person can also feel *malu* if the intensity of the moment does not allow him the opportunity for a light reply.

Children, young adults, adults who are acting as representatives of a family, a school, a business, are routinely and emphatically urged not to bring shame to themselves or others. '*Jangan malu!*' is 'Do your best!' stated inversely.

The westerner may be confused by *malu* because it presupposes that another person can and will feel the same as the wrongdoer.

Most expatriates would dismiss an unpleasant situation breezily with a flippant 'That's your problem!' Do remember that Indonesia is a country of much sharing—of space, goods, and feelings!

Gengsi

This word combines the meanings of 'doing something for the sake of appearances' and 'pretentious behaviour'. Taken to extreme, it can imply a sense of false pride. To be fair, all that *gengsi* implies is surely not original with Indonesia. It is perhaps worth noting that the Indonesians themselves freely label behaviour and projects as *gengsi*. Do a lot of listening to conversations to pick up the meaning of the word before you begin using it.

Asal Bapak Senang

Think of it as 'the source of the father's happiness' or 'whatever makes the boss happy'. Javanese are quick to assert that this philosophy is broadly Indonesian; those from other ethnic backgrounds would suggest that it is a Javanese behaviour.

Learning to speak and act in a pleasing manner begins with the training of children and ultimately becomes part of the national personality. Encountered in the social and business life, *asal bapak senang* means that you can count on your underlings to defer to you. Part of that deference will be telling you whatever they think you want to hear! Forget the facts. 'We want to make you happy.'

At its most gentle, this attitude will spare you embarrassment, provide sometimes undeserved compliments, and give assurances that all is well. At its most pernicious, it manifests itself as hyperbole merging with untruth. It can suggest that saying something will make it happen—building dream castles—whatever seems right to say at the time. In this context, it is possible to read glowing reports about a dreadful situation, e.g. farmers giving enthusiastic reports to officials about projects which are widely known to be in trouble.

Fascinated by this attitude, we asked how factual information reached officials and agents who needed it to implement policy. Privately, so there is no chance of being made *malu*, a trusted adviser will supply the facts to defuse the fantasy.

The foreigner finds this unflattering and frustrating when he is trying to get an evaluation, an assessment, a critique of a programme —situations that are dear to his logical, fact and production-oriented heart. If your Indonesian co-workers perceive that you want a project or speech to be a success, that is what they will tell you! It may take a long time before the facts and true feelings trickle through.

Memojokan

This is social overkill. It implies that a person has been put in a corner and there is no graceful way out nor easy exit, no way to save face in a social situation.

FORGIVENESS

The need to forgive is strong in the Indonesian national ethic. This manifests itself in several ways. It has been systematised at Lebaran when Muslims are obliged to pay duty calls first to their superiors and elders and then to friends, to formally beg forgiveness for their faults and errors of the past year.

The greeting card that is exchanged between friends at that time issues not only the message 'Happy Lebaran'; it also says '*Ma'af Lahir Batin*', pardon all my mistakes.

At Lebaran, expatriates may find their servants on their knees begging forgiveness from the *Tuan* and *Nyonya* for their faults. The words used, 'Please forgive all my mistakes,' indicate a general admission of fault. All the specific errors of the year—the fender dented and unreported, the silver vase bent and put wrinkled-side to the wall, the nylon underwear melted on the iron and put at the bottom of the clothes drawer—are never mentioned in the pursuit of a fresh 'emotional balance sheet'.

Apart from Lebaran, an underling who transgressed in the

The President doing his sungkam to his mother-in-law at Lebaran.

performance of a task in business is expected to report to the superior, admit the fault and offer apology. The boss, who usually already knows all about the situation, will normally either pretend to be surprised by the announcement and accept the apology, or simply accept the apology. The apology must be accepted.

This is more than good manners. It is a ritual that is observed to keep things in balance, to maintain the feeling of harmony in the home, business, or in society.

Accepting apologies for innumerable errors is not license to irresponsibility. Ultimately, reason rules. If more drastic action must be taken against the transgressor it will be done gently, with great attention being paid to avoiding the threat of *malu* (shame). It has also been said that while the Indonesian may forgive they do not forget and they will look for ways to avoid the situation again.

A person of an upper class or status would not offer a formal apology to a member of the lower class, for example, one of the lesser servants in the house or someone who does menial, unskilled labour. Instead, the manner of showing you acknowledge your error is by (1) keeping the social distance intact, and (2) giving small gifts, or (3) trying in other ways to be nice to them. A person of very low status would be acutely embarrassed if he were apologised to. It might be hard for the egalitarian westerner to accept the truth of this, as it functions here.

GHOSTS AND THINGS FEARFUL

Indonesians are both highly spiritual and, for the most part, quick to affirm the presence of spirits. The two are hardly synonymous.

Ghost Stories to Control Children

In all families where it can be afforded, a young child will have a nurse-servant, called a baby-sitter by modern Indonesians. This person, in addition to being responsible for the care of the child, is usually a source of most tales of the supernatural with which she threatens the child into good behaviour.

Some of the ghosts steal children, some cause illness, accidents, or a run of bad luck for the family. Nightmares and irrational fears are common, and in fact most children are afraid to sleep alone or to leave the house in the dark of night.

When asked about the ghost stories and their function of control through fear, one Indonesian parent laughed easily, 'Oh yes, those are the stories we tell our children to threaten them!' For many children throughout the islands, it seems the line between fantasy and fact is thin indeed.

On Java, some of the ghosts are the *sundelbolong*, a frightener of adults, or the *way-way*, a terrifier of small children. That these creatures are never captured and are hesitant to appear to Europeans in no way diminishes their reality to the folk who believe in them.

Leyaks, specialists in the art of black magic and abductors of children, abound in Bali, led by their wild witch queen, Rangda. *Butas* inhabit the sea shores and *kalas* range the thick and shadowed forests. In Sulawesi children stay home at night to avoid the challenge of the *pok-pok*, the flying head!

Many expatriate families have had a child develop a fear of sleeping alone or without a night light. Often the source of these fears is a tale told by the servant. Usually a very brief, calm statement issued to the servant that you would like those stories to STOP will right the situation.

There have also been situations where a family has had a dreadful sequence of disasters or a servant has felt bothered by ghost (*hantu*). Then one may want to deal with the situation in a traditional manner. The afflicted person may choose to consult a *dukun*, a local native-medicine practitioner, or to have a *selamatan*, a religious ceremony of many purposes aimed at restoring calm and balance.

Things Fearful

Indonesians live with the sea, mountains, deserts and volcanoes. How can they not be aware of the truth of the trinity of creation, destruction and preservation? In this awareness, they preserve a balance of calm within and hope to cope with the creation and the destruction without.

They acknowledge the presence of the soul in *pusaka* (heirloom, or sacred weapon/object), trees, rice, flowers, certain animals, hair and fingernail clippings and blood.

The head and the hair are thought to possess quantities of *semangat*, life force. 'We consider our head our crown,' announced a sophisticated Indonesian banker. Casual observation will reveal the head being shielded in many situations. In the rain, people will cover their heads with a plastic sack, a leaf, a piece of paper, or their hands. The head is always lowered to show deference and respect. Traditionally, all persons in a room should keep their heads lower than that of the most honoured person.

Accommodating the Spirits at Home

It is a mistake for the foreigner to view spirit beliefs lightly. Spirits both good and bad are much more part of the scene here than they are in the west. Who is to say what is real? It is enough to acknowledge the reality of the beliefs here.

A sophisticated upper-class Indonesian friend confided that she saw a *hantu*, a spirit, in a tribal mask in a European friend's house. 'I just didn't know what to do,' she said. 'Should I have told her? Those are very dangerous, you know.' Many a western-educated Indonesian doctor has had occasion to refer a patient to *dukun*, men said to be skilled in healing bones and psychiatric disorders.

It is widely believed that the soul can leave the body and travel while the body sleeps. Indonesians are usually very hesitant to wake someone sharply or quickly—the soul is given time to return. Even in a crisis, the manner of waking will be gentle.

Accommodating the Spirits in Business

Goats, chickens and bulls are killed and their heads buried with prayers when major building projects are begun. The sacrifice is to bring good luck, power, blessings, and harmony to the undertaking. Priests are taken by helicopter with a bull's head and other ritual objects to offshore oil rigs and the ceremonies are performed there.

Many books written about Indonesia in general and specific ethnic groups in particular are full of discussions about the Indonesian concern with spirits. If your interest in the subject is genuine, read; if you are merely curious, be gentle in your judgement.

Do/Taboo

- Realise the sacredness of head/hair, especially of small children.
- Respect the need to wake someone gently.
- Resist the temptation to talk someone out of belief in spirits or to belittle that belief.

GOSSIP

Indonesians love to gossip but rarely discuss raw scandal. They seem to know when to stop, and will often protect someone from hearing something that would really hurt him.

Westerners, who are often very sensitive about their personal business and private lives, tend to bridle at the fact that their household staff knows everything that is going on in the home; the office staff is likewise well informed about the business there.

However, the reverse does not always happen. As the *Tuan* or *Nyonya*, it is possible and probable that you will know little about your domestic or business staff. (There is always the possibility that what you do know is only what they thought you would like to hear! See 'Doing Business Indonesian-style', '*Asal Bapak Senang*', and 'The Indonesian Way of Seeing, Doing Honour … with Feeling'.)

The good news is that in the Indonesian communal life ethic a joy or a burden known is a joy or burden shared. The bad news is that expecting secrets to be kept is an investment in frustration.

Vocabulary

Basa basi	Small talk, cocktail party chatter.
Desas-desus (sas-sus)	Light gossip of a harmless nature.
Omong-omong	Conversation, light speech.

NAMES ARE SPECIAL

Throughout Indonesia, names are considered sacred. They can reflect status and social level; the day of birth; the type of work of the father or the family; and the 'cosmic condition' of the person.

A Javanese father will whisper his infant's name to him before it is uttered aloud. Sometimes a Batak mother will name her child after the first object she sees or thinks of after his birth, leaving the child to explain why he is called *payung* (umbrella)!

Among the Javanese, if a series of disasters or illnesses has indicated that the name is *kabotan jeneng* (too heavy), and does not *cocok* (fit) the child, it will be changed. When that happens, it is usual to give the name Slamet, which means 'good luck'.

Some names or name parts hint at occupations of ancestors. Among the Javanese, Tirta indicates a position of civic water management and Sastra reflects a secretarial responsibility.

In the villages, the wife usually keeps her own name at marriage but the children are given the father's name. There is no law that the wife must take her husband's name. However, among the middle classes, this western pattern is now common.

Generally only the Bataks, the Minahasa and some tribes in southern Sulawesi use family names in a manner similar to that in the west.

Among the Minangkabau upper-class families, an adult male will receive an honorary name from the tribe. Names commonly given are Sutan, Bagindo and Datu. In North Sumatra, among the groups that are heavily missionised, one encounters familiar sounding European names. 'My name is an import!' a friend told us.

Some names, such as Pan or Pon or Casino, sound like English words and cause unnecessary confusion. Others are onomatopoeic: Bambang, Bazuki, K'tut, as well as the nicknames Bang and Bung.

Almost all systems of naming—rigid, casual, secret, religious, mystical, long names, names that are only initials, tribal and caste names—are represented in Indonesia.

Javanese Calendar Names

The Javanese still maintain their special calendar, a system of 5 days, *dino pasaran*, that repeats to form a unit of 35 days. The numbers of the 'month' run in sequence from 1 to 35.

Members of the common class identify with both day-name and day-number. Certain important events, one of which is a person's day of birth, are reckoned by those. The careful listener will hear these used as personal names among the villagers: Legi, Paing, Pon, Wage, Kliwon.

Balinese Number Names

The Balinese naming system is far too complicated for the ordinary expatriate to understand completely. However, some aspects can be grasped quickly. It is fun to communicate that understanding to Balinese friends.

Remember that there are three important castes in Bali. The first, the Brahmana, always uses Ida Bagus as a caste identifier in men's names and Ida Ayu in women's. The children are named in the order of their birth: Putu, Made, Nyoman and Ketut.

The next caste, the Satria, does not have number names for the children. Members of the Satria are recognisable by the use of the title Agung Gede in their names.

The Waisa caste uses Ida as a title before a man's name and Ni before a woman's. The children's number names are Wayan, Made, Nyoman and Ketut.

Bapak and Ibu

Many westerners are baffled by the common and obviously honorific use of *Bapak* or *Pak* (father) with men and *Ibu* or *Bu* (mother) with women. Foreigners understandably have trouble shifting these terms into their own culture—imagine a Daddy Bush or a Mother Maggie Thatcher! It helps to know that in a western context, an Indonesian renders these words to their English equivalents: 'Sir' and 'Madam'.

The concept of 'father' has almost mystical overtones for Indonesians and they have a tendency to 'father-fy' almost anyone who possesses higher status and thus greater power than themselves. The whole process of doing honour, passing responsibility, accepting direction seems to be tightly bound in this attitude.

Having just indicated those are words that honour, we must also state that you use them whenever you are addressing someone older or of higher status. (An unmarried, elderly lady will still be addressed as *Ibu* and serious negotiations with the aged vegetable seller will be prefaced by *Pak*.)

Being Comfortable with Indonesian Names

When you hear a name for the first time, it is permissible to ask that it be repeated. Try saying it back, 'It is nice to meet you, Mr _____.' If you are given a calling card, write the name as it sounds to you on the back so you can remember it. Indonesian names are pronounceable if you break them into rhythmic syllables.

Common people usually have only one name; members of the middle class will often have two, roughly equivalent to the western first and last names); members of the upper class will have long names. They often prefer to use a shortened name and an initial. In that case, Deddy B. would be addressed as Bapak Deddy.

On Java, Mas (gold) is also used as a familiar form of address for men. You will often hear it used in a setting roughly similar to the appropriate use of Mate, Squire, Bloke and Pal. (Formal titles and introductions are discussed in 'The Social Circle, Making Introductions'.) New acquaintances and children will always use what they assume to be the respectful title. It is a 'gift of time' to call someone by his or her intimate name. Therefore, if the Indonesians say 'Mrs Sally' or 'Mr Bob', it is their respectful rendering of the names and not an assumed intimacy.

After all our warnings about social rigidity, be prepared for young people. This does not imply great intimacy or close friendship. They assume it to be correct manners. And usually that is just fine.

Honorific titles from various ethnic groups are often added to or used in lieu of 'call names'. For example, Daud and Teuku are titles from northern Sumatra; Raden and Raden Mas are Javanese/Sundanese titles; Andi is a Bugis title; Ida Bagus is from Bali and Tubagus is from Bantam (north Java).

Using 'Call Names' Correctly

Indonesians don't spend much time clearing throats to attract attention or ask for service. Instead, they use the 'call names' that are appropriate within the various ethnic groups.

Balinese

Geg   Abbreviation of *egeg* (pretty). Addressing a young woman.
Gus   Abbreviation of *bagus* (good). Addressing a man.

Batak

Amang   Addressing an older man. Equivalent to *Bapak*.
Eda   Term of address between women.
Inang   Addressing an older woman. Equivalent to *Ibu*.
Ito   Woman addressing a man, or vice versa.
Lae   Term of address between men.

Javanese

Bapak   Term of highest honour for men throughout the country.
Bung   Term of address between men, as in 'Hey, you (friend)', popular during the struggle for independence by Sukarno.
Ibu   Term of highest honour for women throughout the country.
Mas   Addressing a man.
Sus   Addressing a woman of a lower social position. Non-specific.

Minangkabau

Bayung   Addressing a man.
Upik   Addressing a woman.

Sundanese

Jang   Addressing a young man or boy of the same generation.
Mang   Addressing an older man a generation or more older than the speaker.
Neng   Addressing a young girl.
Nyai   Term often used by an older woman to describe herself. In colonial times it was an unflattering word describing a European's Indonesian mistress. Nowadays, it usually means 'old woman'.

PANCASILA

Pancasila is the term for five principles constituting the state philosophy of Indonesians, the doctrine upon which government is based. The preamble to the 1945 constitution states clearly 'belief in One, Supreme God, a just and civilised Humanity, the unity of Indonesia, democracy which is guided by the inner wisdom in the unanimity arising out of deliberation amongst representatives … creating a condition of social justice for the whole of the people of Indonesia.' The efficacy and strength of *Pancasila* for maintaining stability and moderation in the affairs of the country are widely acknowledged. The world press credited *Pancasila* with supporting the principle of freedom of religion in Indonesia and national political leaders have referred to *Pancasila* as a force for moderation and consensus government, and a curb against extreme ideologies.

The P-4 Orientation

It is considered very much in the interests of the Indonesian people to understand the constitution and the principles of *Pancasila*. Therefore, all government employees, persons in government-related businesses, educators, and junior high, high school and university students enrol in the P-4 Programme, a week's intensive orientation.

The P-4 is comprised of *Pendidikan* (education), *Penghayatan* (understanding of the *Pancasila*), *Pengamalan* (application of *Pancasila* in everyday life) and the *Pancasila* (understanding the five principles). In addition, during the course, the participants study the constitution, the national goals, the Five-Year Development Plans (usually expressed in a programme called Pelita I-V), national consciousness, and flag etiquette.

PRESSURE

Social behaviour is controlled and influenced through various forms of unsubtle pressure. If, for example, a young person is behaving in a way that displeases the family, favoured older relatives will begin to 'drop in' and just happen to discuss the issue in a rather oblique fashion. In this way the misbehaving individual is exposed to a person he admires and to whom he owes respect because of age. Often used as leverage is the possibility of *malu*, shame and the feeling that one owes good behaviour.

The expatriate may find a similar pressure being placed upon him, usually by members of the household staff. If there is a situation being negotiated—termination of work due to pregnancy, or the possibility of money being loaned for buying land, building a house, school fees—it is not uncommon for another servant to 'drop in' and begin to speak about another employer's generosity on the same issue. If successful, this provokes great guilt in the heart of the expatriate.

Guiding Ideas
The government *Pancasila* course (P-4) is part of a programme to teach awareness and responsibility to the national goals. (See '*Pancasila*', opposite.)

Looking and behaving in a uniform manner ('fitting in', being part of the group) is highly valued. Group courses, group uniforms, large group activities all reinforce this and, in theory, assist in identifying with the national goals. For example, the government physical fitness programme determines that each week civil servants and other groups perform group exercises together, often in matching sweatsuits. You may also see thousands of people gathered in the early morning for special highly organised mass jogging, cycling, or other events.

Group Socialising
In a country as densely populated as Indonesia, it is probably just as well that people get used to doing almost everything as part of a group. 'There is no such thing as private business, property, or time,' remarked a friend.

91

Being part of a group serves as a form of social discipline for teenagers, and is thought to provide safety and security for all. The solitary condition is considered personally dangerous and emotionally undesirable. Solitary behaviour in the sense that it is creative, individual, unique—words that cause the foreigner's blood to race—is not highly valued. Housemaids will find a friend just to accompany them on errands. Patients are visited by car-loads of relatives. Entire villages will load into buses and trucks to send off those going to make the pilgrimage to Mecca. They fill the floor space at airports, eating and sleeping until the moment of departure is shared by all.

Each person is very much his brother's keeper (also provider, mother, adviser, father, brother, mentor, judge, companion, friend, confidante, resource, ally, playmate, pal).

Teasing

It is desirable that each person feel as one with the group. One of the ways the individual is conditioned for communal living is by teasing.

This was described by a young Indonesian lad to his friend as '... a game. Everyone tries to get on your nerves. You lose if you show a reaction! You win if you can give the appearance of not caring.' It is a subtle and strong method of achieving at least the appearance of 'inner calm'.

Alert foreigners will observe much teasing of this nature among all age groups. It can be cruel if it is aimed at the handicapped or the unknowing. Young expatriate children sometimes have difficulty with this. It also seems to contradict the Indonesians' known love of children. It might help a little to know that some of the teasing that expatriates feel is aimed at them exclusively is also aimed with equal enthusiasm at other Indonesians.

SEX, LOVE AND SWEATY ENCOUNTERS

The world's oldest profession is practised in Indonesia. Transvestites lurk on street corners and hiss sweetly, 'Hello, baby ...' There are deep-voiced hairdressers with 'five o'clock shadows' visible under layers of pancake make-up, bar-girls, whores who set up shop under large beach umbrellas and elegant kept women. They are all here.

They exist alongside some very strict *adat* (traditional law) regarding dealings with women. In times not too far past, *adat* allowed an Achenese father to stone his daughter if she dallied with a man before she married.

It is worth noting that men of all social classes typically walk holding hands or with arms interlocked. Women do it to a lesser degree. This is not a statement about widespread homosexuality; rather it reflects the Indonesian's sense of personal space. Do not conclude that because they touch each other a lot, that you may.

Indonesia emphatically does not have and does not want the reputation of having 'sin cities'. The government is interested in marketing sunny beaches, glorious monuments and interaction with cultures that genuinely prize and practise modest and chaste behaviour and speech, the Indonesian virtues of *kesopan* and *santunan*.

Organised Prostitution

The official government policy is against organised prostitution. However, it exists. Dolly and Charak are well known red-light districts in Surabaya, East Java. Pucok in Jambi (east Sumatra) has the dubious reputation of being one of the best run prostitution villages in Indonesia. Operating for almost 40 years, Pucok is entirely self-governing and has its own city officials. Several hundred women mostly from Java serve the sailors, truck drivers and other labourers. According to an account in one of Jakarta's popular daily newspapers, Pucok was the site of an airlift that has become almost legend. A supervisor of a jungle-bound work crew arranged for his men to be flown to the village and then out in time to work the next morning.

In the cities, the bar-girls, attendants in massage parlours, entertainers in nightclubs and flocks of elegant secretaries (deservedly or not) are the focus of much of the interest in sex-for-sale.

(Above) The lovely jamu (native medicine) sellers from Central Java have steady customers for the tonics they sell. (Left) The butterflies of the evening hang around street corners to solicit customers.

The spread of information about family planning, increased exposure to other literature, movies, television and travel abroad have all served to rearrange some of the traditional attitudes about sex and sexuality.

Sex and the Villager

Attitudes toward recreational sex in Indonesia are conveniently grouped by socio-economic categories. The behaviour and speech of the lower class Indonesians are generally acknowledged to be crude and earthy. Some of the characters in the *wayang kulit* (puppet plays) reflect this. The supposed ideal behaviour for a villager is to be sexless until marriage and then to produce many children.

Street-side and market hawkers of native medicine—men with collections of pills and the Javanese *jamu* ladies with their bottles of homemade herbal drinks—usually peddle elixirs that promise to make the male powerful and enduring and the female overreach the local sex standards. Some of these sales are enhanced by visual aids that can only be described as wishful. There is a compendium of local lore, both black and white magic, native medicines, fact and fancy associated with sexual strength, allure and behaviour.

Not unrelated to this is the fact that, for many villagers, as many living children as possible is the best family insurance. There is a vested interest in producing children. The government is providing broader health services and childcare clinics so people will be satisfied with smaller, healthy families.

For most villagers, the awakening of hormonal urges is handled by early marriage. The fact that few of these marriages last, that couples are recycled and children farmed out to the greater family seems to be regarded as a separate issue from one's sexual behaviour.

Some of the local newspapers are a treasure of florid reporting of creative trysts in the villages. The stories that entertain most expatriates describe angry, cuckolded husbands pursuing the interloper with a knife to lop off the offending organ.

Hukum Karma

What of the Indonesian wife who discovers that she has competition? If lower-class, she could pursue the offender with a knife; the middle-class woman would probably seek a divorce, separation, or return to her family; the upper class woman who wishes to continue enjoying the perks of her lifestyle may merely invoke the damning power of *hukum karma*.

Hukum karma is a dread oath that is often thought, rarely said, and usually related to (unhappy) affairs of the heart. It calls down the law of *karma* on the head of the offender with the earnest wish that 'You'll get yours!'

Holding to the belief in the power of *hukum karma* provides a sense of divine retribution for wives whose husbands are keeping mistresses or having affairs. The oath is not uttered lightly.

'Indos'

Because of Indonesia's long association with travellers and business-men from abroad, there are many families of mixed parentage. In the past the word 'Indo' used only to refer to the offspring of an Indonesian mother and a European father. In some areas the careless use of this word (which seems to uninformed foreigners a logical abbreviation of 'Indonesian') is a sensitive issue.

Unfortunately, the folk tradition of the European planter who felt he needed only three things to be happy in Indonesia while away from his family in Europe—his *nasi goreng* (fried rice), *sambal* (chilli paste) and his *nyai* (mistress)—overcast those many instances of lasting and affectionate mixed marriages.

It is important to remember that most Indonesians are modest and have no desire to deviate from their traditional, correct, chaste behaviour.

Vocabulary

Banci	Slang for transvestite.
Cewek	'Chick', a 'cool' modern girl.
Cowok	'Dude', a 'with-it' young man.
Gundik	Mistress.
Hukum karma	You'll get yours! This is thought, not said. It is a very negative remark associated with divine revenge, often invoked in affairs of the heart.
Main cewek	Literally, 'to play with women'. Equivalent to 'looking for some action' or 'cruising'.
Nona	Miss, unmarried woman.
Nonya	Party-girl, as understood in the west. Pronounced with heavy emphasis on the long *o* sound.
Nyonya	Polite and correct term for a married woman. Pronounced with emphasis on the *ny* sound.
Pacar	Girlfriend or boyfriend.
Pelacur	Polite term for prostitute.
Perek	Slang for whore.
Wadam	Transvestite.
White hunters	Women who hang around bars, hoping to pick up expatriate men (intention: marriage).
W.T.S.	*Wanita tuna susila* (woman without morals); whore.

TIME ... RUBBER AND OTHERWISE

The 24-hour day is divided into four sections:

pagi	roughly midnight to 11 a.m.
siang	11 a.m. to 3 p.m.
sore	3 to 6:45 p.m.
malam	6:45 p.m. to midnight

To be clear, one would say '*jam dua pagi*' for two o'clock in the morning, and '*jam dua siang*' for two o'clock in the afternoon. Repeated time words like *pagi-pagi* or *malam-malam* suggest very early or very late.

Interestingly enough, this pattern of the division of the day was remarked upon by Sir Stamford Raffles when he served in Java as Lt. Governor in the early 1800s. He noticed that generally people rose for the early (*pagi*) prayers and began work immediately after that, ate and slept during the heat of the day (*siang*), worked again in the cool of the afternoon (*sore*), and ate and spent time with family and friends during *malam*. Outside the airconditioned offices of the cities, this pattern is still practised. You might also encounter it in the work habits of your domestic staff!

Indonesians are very familiar with the 24-hour clock for ticket reservations and official printed invitations to parties. However, between friends, the *pagi*, *siang*, *sore*, *malam* expression of time is used. An invitation for Sunday night would be expressed as *Minggu malam Senin* (Sunday evening before Monday).

Time Reckoning

The seven-day week is only one of several time divisions that Indonesians use. The Balinese have their Hindu calendar, the Muslims their Islamic calendar.

Then there are the market days. In the villages throughout the islands the five-day market week system is still in operation. In the larger towns one encounters only the names of these old markets: *Pasar Rebu* (Wednesday Market), *Pasar Senin* (Monday Market), *Pasar Minggu* (Sunday Market), *Pasar Juma'at* (Friday Market) and *Pasar Selasa* (Tuesday Market).

Throughout the country, there are also morning markets, *pasar pagi*, for fresh foods. Time is reckoned by these for everyone knows that the market begins right after morning prayer and is finished by 10 a.m.! The night markets, *pasar malam*, can have all the flavour and fun of a local fair, carnival, or bazaar. They do not open until after the evening prayer at sundown and they are at their fullest after 8 p.m. In the larger cities they are usually the venue for the street-food stalls, clothing and shoe markets, and music cassettes.

Rubber Time

Jam karet or rubber time is a phrase of convenience that asks forgiveness for a multitude of sins. It expresses a remarkably laid-back approach to punctuality. In its most gracious translation, it would correspond to 'about ____ o'clock'. In its most rubberised form, it would allow a tardiness of several hours. At its most reasonable, it acknowledges the delays caused by traffic snarls, bad roads, missing bridges, or any of a thousand obstacles that Indonesia can produce to prevent punctuality.

There are three important exceptions to all that we have said above.

1. The expatriate is expected to arrive promptly if he is given an appointment by someone of higher status than he. (Doing honour to a person of higher status is involved here as well as the fact that Indonesians know that punctuality is important in the western world.)

2. In the highest Indonesian social and business circles, the invitations usually state clearly, *Mohon hadir 15 minit sebelumnya* (Arrive 15 minutes early). Sometimes the guests are asked to be half an hour early. Do observe that! It is never stated but always understood that at these events it is probable that you will have to 'hurry up to wait'.

3. Permeating the culture, but especially obvious with the lower classes and domestic staff, is the impression that they are not driven by time unless there is an emergency with their own family ... a death call, someone ill or injured. In those cases, they plan, pack, ask for money and depart with a velocity usually reserved for light.

Chapter Six

THE SOCIAL CIRCLE

The social fabric of Indonesia is as rich, varied and significant as its textile fabrics. The foreigner may find himself at times absorbed into this complex pattern and at other times given the place of observer.

We offer some suggestions to help you be comfortable with formal introductions, and appropriate small talk; to host Indonesian counterparts in your home, with notes on some differences in entertaining styles; and to understand situations you might encounter in an Indonesian friend's home. The social pressures familiar to most middle-class Indonesians are discussed. The *arisan*, a favoured form of socialising, is contrasted with the cocktail party. A list of official holidays is included. Some facts about Islam that the foreigner will observe are given.

Indonesians spend a great deal of time keeping their social lives in order in the context of their communal lifestyle. The foreigner who understands this will have an understanding of both the pleasure and the emotional support that socialising gives to Indonesians.

MAKING INTRODUCTIONS

You can tell the correct social status of a person by the manner of the introduction.

Very traditional Indonesians appreciate including as many titles and designations of the person who is being introduced as possible so as to avoid leaving out any information that would cause embarrassment. It is possible you will hear yourself saying, 'May I introduce His Excellency Professor Dr Ambassador X!'

Most of the Indonesians who have travelled widely or been educated overseas adopt the western manner of handling introductions. Some do not routinely use their academic titles.

It is all right to introduce yourself or to ask for somebody's name. It is also permissible to ask that a third party introduce you.

Doing It Right

Here is the formula for the most formal introduction. One begins with the words for 'I would like to present ...' and then supplies the information more or less in this order:

1. *Bapak/Ibu* +
2. academic title if applicable +
3. noble title if the person routinely uses it +
4. person's given and family names +
5. business and social position +
6. academic title if you did not use it at the beginning.

Words to Say

Bapak	Sir. This would be the term used to introduce any male of rank, from the President down. It precedes any other title he may have.
Drs	Abbreviation of *Doktorandus*, accorded a male graduate in any field except engineering or law. Formerly the Dutch title for a person who had completed the residence work for a Ph.D. but not the dissertation.
Dra.	*Doktoranda*, feminine of *Doktorandus*.
Ibu	Madam, the correct address for all women. It precedes any other title she possesses.
Ingin (Boleh) saya memperkenalkan ...	I would like to present ...
Ir.	Abbreviation for *Insinjur*, the title for one who has received an engineering degree in the Netherlands or Indonesia.
Isteri	Wife (of). The 'of' is implied.
S. Econ.	Abbreviation of *Sarjana Economics*, a graduate of the School of Economics.
S.H.	Abbreviation of *Sarjana Hukum*, a graduate of the Law Faculty.
S.S.	Abbreviation of *Sarjana Sastra*, a graduate of the Faculty of Letters.
Suami	Husband (of). The 'of' is implied.

When all else fails, remember that Indonesians are highly skilled at spotting and responding to genuineness in others. Your own honest pleasure and enthusiasm in meeting people will carry the day and there is no need to get in a twist about proper titles.

RULES OF SOCIAL CONVERSATION

It is one of life's great truths that we are judged by what we say. And trying to be relaxed and effective while communicating information, ideas and feelings in a foreign language requires a healthy dose of courage and patience.

Expatriates and probably Indonesians as well sometimes ridicule the standard cocktail party and morning tea (non)conversations … Where are you from? How long have you been here? How many children? etc. *ad nauseum*. However, those statements are crucial in the sequence of becoming acquainted and are found in all cultures. Therefore, let us not respond limply to an opportunity to lay a foundation for real friendship.

We include some specific information to guide you through beginning conversations and point out areas where Indonesians are prepared to speak easily.

Inviting Conversation

In traditional Indonesian society, if a person is not involved in a conversation or invited to join it, he may not participate in it. Therefore, it might be difficult for an Indonesian to initiate a conversation. He is usually relieved to be spoken to. As you practise the gentle art of conversation in Indonesia, consider these points:

1. Get the personal data first.

People expect such an opening line and are prepared for it. If you are speaking with *pasar* shopkeepers or *kampung tukangs* you ask, 'What is your *kampung* or village?' If you are speaking with counterparts and members of the middle class, you would say, 'What is your *asal* or *daerah*?' The answer should be an area in Indonesia or the name of a city. At that point, because you have read a little about Indonesian history (streets, page 30), food (page 51) and people (ethnic sketches, page 17), you are prepared to make intelligent conversation.

103

Asal	Origin or source. Foreigners are often asked, '*Asal di mana?*' What is your country of origin? This is used in preference to *negeri*: country or land.
Daerah	Territory or region.
Kampung	Understood to mean rural village; also an area in a city. *Kampungan* or country bumpkin implies lack of sophistication.
Tukang	Usually a workman or skilled labourer. While it may mean artisan in the sense of *tukang kayu* (carpenter or wood carver), it usually means 'one who does ...'. It is contrasted with *ahli* which means excellent, competent.

2. Pay attention to their name.

Does it give you a clue to their ethnic group? Take a chance! If you hear 'Mrs Widodo' ask, 'Are you from Central Java?'

Are husband and wife from the same area? Marriages between ethnic groups are considered very modern. An acceptable query is, 'Did you have problems adjusting to the two cultures?' An Indonesian friend told us, 'When you know someone well you can ask anything!'

3. Get the data about the family.

'Ask us about our children,' urged an Indonesian friend. There is nothing wrong with the standard questions: How many children? How old are they? This is your chance to tell her how young she looks to be a mother.

4. Do not bluntly ask about age.

Everyone wants to know! Most women prepare standard answers. One response is a light smile and '*Senja*' (twilight). Another is, 'My hair is old (grey) but my heart is young!' Yet another is to be blatantly ridiculous. For example, to the statement, 'My, you don't look old enough to have a son 21!' you could respond with a smile that makes it clear you are joking, 'I had him when I was 8.'

5. Choose the right time to pay compliments.

When western women first greet each other they usually spend a lot of time remarking on their clothes, choice of colours, etc. Indonesian women are renowned for their beauty and certainly prepare to look their best. However, they do not expect a first meeting to be an occasion for compliments unless the garment is exceptional, in the sense of a costume. If an Indonesian lady were complimented, she would be pleased, accept the compliment, but would not expect it.

6. Voice your feelings.

It is all right and sometimes necessary to be able to say both 'Yes, I like it here' and 'I miss my family and children in ...' Indonesians are deeply attached to their families and would understand that comment. It builds a bridge of commonality. Indonesian professionals are often transferred around the country. Many have said that a move from Jakarta to Acheh or Yogyakarta to Kalimantan, or Jakarta to Sulawesi is like an overseas posting.

7. Inquire about interests and travel.

Given the government emphasis on physical fitness and sport, recreational interests is a good topic. Indonesians who travel or have been educated overseas enjoy sharing those experiences.

8. Be sensitive to their international travel experiences.

Stifle the urge to respond to their impressions of Las Vegas with a riotous tale of how many thousand dollars you lost or won there. Allow them the totality of their experience and do not overwhelm it with one of your own. Among lower middle-class Indonesians, domestic travel is usually in response to deaths in the family and rarely for pleasure. The expatriate who has been in Indonesia for two to three years may have seen more of the country than most of his Indonesian counterparts and friends.

9. Expect birth control to crop up in conversation.

Indonesians speak with little inhibition about birth control and related issues because there is such emphasis on it. Educating the people to limit their families is a major governmental concern. The early days of the family planning programme produced some classic posters. Still fondly remembered was a huge signboard near the centre of Jakarta that asked the world: 'Has *Bapak* worn his condom today?'

Recently couples that became family planning 'acceptors' were given coconut seedlings by the government. The fact that coconuts are highly valued agriculturally was obscured amid giggles provided by the image of the farmer with his coconuts.

Condoms and coconuts aside, it is quite another situation to find yourself involved in a social conversation on these topics. Secretaries in the office will announce with candour, 'Well, that's the second child. Now I use an IUD.'

10. Don't introduce business into social occasions.

There are very strong feelings among the old and traditional businessmen that the office is the place for business. It is sometimes felt that any inquiry about the job or work in a social setting is ultimately going to lead to an attempt to do business. Many people are uncomfortable with that and the conversation may sag.

The obvious exception is when you are invited to a formal reception to welcome a visiting dignitary. Then, it is correct and easiest to inquire about business matters, since that is the purpose of the visit. Conversational topics are largely decided by the nature of the event.

Do not count on an informative response to an inquiry about the job. The same answer would be given by everyone, from the office boy to the director of the company: 'I work at …'

Being a Cultural Commentator

Indonesians are extremely proud of their country. Energetic nationalism is encouraged. But do not expect them to be commentators on the culture or make the mistake of seeing them as ethnic representatives rather than as interesting individuals. Just as not every Thai grew up grooming elephants, neither did every Indonesian lad ride caribou and pose for wood carvings. Most of your Indonesian counterparts are well educated, highly travelled, aware and fascinating to know.

Cultural differences among expatriates may not be easily recognised by many Indonesians. There is the possibility that an individual expatriate will be seen as arch-typical of his country, a true representative. This lays expectations and responsibilities on the expatriate that he may be unaware of and not welcome.

Therefore, remember the foreign resident in Indonesia always:
- has a responsibility to be a gracious guest even when he is a host in his own home here, and
- is seen as a representative of his country and his country's policies.

1. Learn to interpret laughter.

If in the conversation you hear an inappropriate laugh or giggle, you will know that the talk has derailed and your conversation partner is confused or not understanding. Do not ask, 'What's funny about that?' Rephrase and start over. Don't confuse the nervous laugh with a laugh of pleasure. You will quickly learn the difference!

2. Inject humour in conversation.

Remember that a sense of humour bridges all cultural gaps. Much that is unfamiliar to the foreigner can also be riotously funny. Indonesians are delighted with the foreigner who can laugh at himself. The Indonesian phrase for small talk is extremely apt: *basa basi* (empty words). No one expects to have a 'meaningful conversation'. It is light, superficial, and fills the time.

107

Indonesian Expectations

Indonesians would appreciate hearing:

1. That you have acquired some skill with the language.

They may apologise for their poor English which is often very good. They will also praise the foreigner's skill in Bahasa Indonesia even if it is meagre.

2. That you appreciate some of the foods.

The foreigner is expected to like the *saté* and the fried rice and allowed to recoil when asked about the odiferous fruit, durian. To confess a fondness for some of the lesser known traditional foods is to win instant friends.

3. That you and your family like it here.

Respond positively to the query, 'How do you find Indonesia?' Acknowledge the great beauty of the country before you mutter about overpopulation. Enthuse about the abundance of fantastic fruit and inexpensive flowers before you grumble about the traffic. This is not the time to go into detail about your plumbing problems, red tape in doing business, the heat, cats and rats that romp on your roof, and static on the phone. Neither would they be interested in your plan to lay land mines at traffic circles to solve traffic problems. All these and more exist for Indonesians, too. Yet to them being in Indonesia is the most wonderful of all situations in the world. A bitter and blatant negative response from an expatriate would leave the inquirer wondering, 'Why in the world are you here?'

4. That you find them friendly and helpful.

Indonesians smile a lot. They like to be smiled at and appreciate at least the illusion of friendliness and calm that this creates. They think of themselves as polite, friendly and eager to please and they are absolutely correct.

**5 That you find the national dress and the traditional
fabrics and handicrafts attractive.**
That does not mean you have to rush out and have all your tennis
socks *batik*ed or put in an order for *ikat* (handwoven) underwear.
Simply remember to comment positively on the things that are a
source of national pride.

Terminating the Conversation

An abrupt answer means, STOP! enough. If you answer abruptly
and without a smile, you are dismissing, literally. The gentler exit is
a smile and the formula-word, '*Permisi* ...' as you leave the group.
It means 'excuse me' and asks permission to leave.

DESCRIBING BEHAVIOUR

The suggestion that Indonesians live in 30 centuries at once is valid
if one compares the stone-age tribesmen of Irian Jaya with the high-
tech aspects of urban life. It is equally, but less obviously, true if one
looks to the manifestations of ancient beliefs that survive in the
wayang kulit, the famous shadow play of Indonesia. Briefly, it is
thought that the shadow—with its two-dimensional aspect—was
used as the vehicle for teaching esoteric knowledge and religion.
(There is a mass of literature on the subject.)

Scholars feel that the *wayang* was common in Java before the
arrival of the Hindus because of the presence of Semar, a pre-Hindu
figure, in the cast of characters. In addition to absorbing much of the
Hindu philosophy as stated in the epics, the *Ramayana* and the
Mahabharata, the *wayang kulit* plays enforce and illustrate the
importance of society as a whole, whose harmonious order guarantees
the right and quiet life of its members. An individual's life is public
and should give (at least) the appearance of control, self-discipline.
To yield to harmonious general order it is better to do nothing than
stimulate a situation that could cause disorder; it is better to be
content with little than to strive to be ambitious.

The personalities of the *wayang* characters are so well known that mentioning them is a common method for describing an individual. The statement, 'He is like Ardjuna' would immediately suggest a good-looking, loyal, self-confident, brave, 'smooth' male, possessed of spiritual strength. To describe a man as a real Gatot Kaca would suggest physical strength and 'macho' maleness manifested in size and hirsute appearance, bravery, loyalty and a willingness to defend himself and others. In addition, Gatot Kaca has the mystical ability to 'rise above' (he can fly) and see a situation from an altered perspective. To say a person is a Rahwana is to imply in one word that he is a bum, greedy, evil, without scruples, disloyal, and a general all-time loser.

Super Semar is the term by which Indonesians describe the Surat Perintah Sebelas Maret, the decree of 11 March 1966 when an ailing Sukarno handed over the powers of government to General (now President) Suharto. If one knows that Semar is the oldest of the Javanese *wayang* characters and one of great power and respect, the nickname enhances the power of the decree.

Realising that how one behaves is important, here are the words that you will hear and use to describe people and their behaviour.

Baik hati	Good-hearted, a 'soft touch'.
Baik kelakuannya	Well-behaved.
Bandal	Mischievous.
Cemberut	Sombre.
Cerewet	Talkative, a blabbermouth.
Halus	Refined and elegant behaviour.
Jahat	Not nice, rotten, bad.
Jelek	Rotten.
Kasar	Crude, rough.
Keras hati	Stubborn, persistent.
Kurang ajar	Ill-mannered, the strongest possible polite way of criticising someone's behaviour.
Lincah	Energetic.

Lucu	Funny.
Nakal	Naughty.
Pemberani (Berani)	Brave.
Pemalu (Malu)	Shy.
Ramah	Friendly.
Sabar	Patient.
Sopan	Respectful and decent.

ENTERTAINING INDONESIAN COUNTERPARTS

If it is true that many Indonesians find the cocktail party a bit of a chore, most do enjoy being invited into their counterparts' homes. Every hostess who has the opportunity to entertain in her home wants the evening to be comfortable and enjoyable for all. We offer brief guidelines.

Plan your dinner for a Saturday or Sunday evening. Send written invitations addressed to both the husband and wife about a week ahead of time. If the invitation says 'From 7, or 7–9', the guests will know that it means dinner. Most of the guests will arrive about half an hour late, which is considered 'on time'. Muslims observe the *maghrib* prayers at about 7:30 and then eat.

As the guests arrive and are settled, serve them a selection of chilled soft drinks and juice (no ice) in small glasses from a tray. It is possible that drinks will only be sipped and not totally consumed. Alcohol is not widely used. Include cocktail napkins on the tray, but do not be surprised if not everyone takes one. Nuts and small fried Indonesian snacks on small plates must be served otherwise no one will help himself.

Your guests will expect about an hour of small talk before the meal. Many Indonesian men and usually most of the wives are uncomfortable about their ability to converse in a language other than Bahasa Indonesia. Indonesians are quite comfortable with the idea of sitting silently.

It is as necessary for the hostess as for the other guests to know

111

who is the ranking or more honoured guest. That person will begin the buffet line. The host or hostess should accompany him or her through the line and explain the special dishes served.

Indonesians are most comfortable with a meal presented as a buffet. Stack dishes on the sideboard but set places to around tables. See 'Menus that Work' for meal suggestions. If you have enough staff, they can pass the food around for seconds. Otherwise, invite guests to help themselves. When you are sure everyone has finished, tables may be cleared and the party moved to the living-room.

Coffee and tea are served from a trolley or tray and each guest is expected to help himself to sugar or cream. Your guests will know that the evening is over when the coffee is served. Soon you will begin to hear the formula-word, '*Permisi ...*' ('I beg your pardon, but it is time to leave.') Expect each guest to offer the gentle handshake at departure. If it is possible, escort your honoured guests to their car. The evening rarely lasts beyond 9 or 9:30 p.m.

MENUS THAT WORK

'We like to be told what the foreign hostess is going to serve. That way we can save space if there is something truly yummy!' joked an Indonesian friend. Another added, 'I like to know because if I have never had it before or I don't like it ... I can eat at home first.'

It is helpful for most expatriates to reflect that they probably learnt to eat the Indonesian foods that their own household staff eat. That food is flavourful and inexpensive and there is every reason to eat it and enjoy it. However, do not make the error of serving it to sophisticated Indonesian guests. One foreigner unthinkingly made the mistake and his guest was heard to mutter, 'This is *makanan belakang.*' (This is servants' food.)

Soups

Thick cream soups (meat or vegetable). Special favourites are mushroom, chicken, tomato, pea and bean soups.

Vegetables

Cap cay (*chap chai*) or other stir-fried vegetables are always well received. Canned sweetcorn is a favourite as is almost any creamed vegetable casserole. Young vegetables pan-fried in butter is an easy way to please most guests. Potato salad (hot or cold) is an item on the menu inherited from the Dutch and much enjoyed.

Main Courses

Always check the dietary restrictions of your guests. Rice for most people is really the main course. All the other foods are side dishes.

Meat served in the following manner is usually successful: beef/ mushroom stew similar to stroganoff; pasta with ground beef in tomato sauce similar to lasagne; cold sliced beef, chicken or turkey; beef or chicken curry; beef/noodle casserole with sour cream; *rendang* (beef cooked in coconut cream and spices); roullade (stuffed meat roll); macaroni, cheese and ham (to non-Muslims); smoked tongue with peas in white sauce; *semur* (oven-top stew or casserole); chicken and beef *saté*.

A complete menu for a typical Indonesian meal would feature fried rice, fried noodles, chicken *saté*, chicken curry, beef stew or sliced fillet, baked or scalloped potatoes, a potato salad, pickles and shrimp crackers.

Breads

Serve sliced French bread or small dinner rolls.

Desserts

Chocolate cake with 'gloppy' rich frosting, fruit cake, chocolate mousse or puddings and western fruit pies are all usually enjoyed. Fruit salad or fresh fruit is considered mandatory.

In addition, foreigners have found that regional dishes (Mexican or Italian, for example) or traditional national holiday fare are

113

usually well received. When Indonesians entertain, the menu is limited and the amount of food generous. It is well to follow that lead and provide ample amounts of a selected menu.

MAJOR DIFFERENCES IN ENTERTAINING

You will encounter at least three significant areas of difference between traditional western and traditional Indonesian entertaining. The first of these is the purpose of the social meal, the second is the open-ended guest list and the third is the role played by the food.

The Purpose of the Social Meal

The western idea of inviting friends to one's home to share a meal for the pleasure of their company or inviting a couple in 'to get to know them' contrasts with the general Indonesian concept that a party should have a specific and traditional purpose like a wedding or a religious event. Indonesians may well ask 'Why?' in response to your invitation.

They will also try to discover who the guest of honour is, necessary information for them as it determines their behaviour. In addition, they hope to hear the names of the other guests because many Indonesians do not like being invited as a single couple to an expatriate's home. Because they are concerned about keeping up conversation, they are happier as part of a larger group where they can converse superficially and move from person to person.

The Open-ended Guest List

The westerner is comfortable planning a party precisely—limiting the space at the tables, or restricting the gathering to a set number. From the Indonesian viewpoint, this would not only be difficult, but rude. It could exclude someone who might want to come or make it awkward for an invitee to bring a friend. It is important to convey that all are welcome. Generally, it is a cultural value to be inclusive rather than exclusive and one must be open to changes in planning.

RSV...what? There is no cultural need to respond formally to invitations. Indeed, even when Indonesians wish to, it may not be easy for them. It is possible that there is not a phone available, or the phone does not work, or they must react quickly to a totally different situation: a death, a friend dropping in, a relative with a pressing need. One never knows! In fact the host or hostess may not know exactly who is coming until the guests actually arrive.

A group of expatriates were sharing tales of party-planning paranoia and the feeling was growing that the unpredictability of the guest list was a plot by those desiring to confuse and distress the well-meaning westerner. The situation lightened when one woman recounted a very lovely dinner at a posh restaurant in Jakarta hosted by an Indonesian couple. As the guests were enjoying a pre-dinner cocktail, a hurried exchange was noted between the maitre D' and the hostess. It became obvious that some of the guests were not going to come. Tables were hastily rearranged. After hearing the tale, the expatriate wives realised the very situations that confuse them are equally distressing to the Indonesian hostess.

Incidentally, this unpredictability makes the buffet dinner a very comfortable and low-risk way to entertain.

Not only is there no cultural need to reply to invitations, Indonesian friends tell us that in the process of planning there is a subtle shifting away from the sense of personal responsibility. If there were a change in plans, it would not be the fault of the invitee. One woman remarked that even if she invited her best friend to come to her house for dinner, she knows her friend would reply and mean '*Insya Allah*' (If God wills it). There is no blame laid, except on fate! Don't plan too precisely or make bargains with the future.

Of course, as guests, sophisticated Indonesians who have lived abroad or have had wide business and diplomatic experience will be comfortable with the western system of RSVP and the detailed planning of parties. As hosts, they will always make an effort to find out how many might come to their party and then prepare for a few

115

more. But the western compulsion to know all the details beforehand is weak in the Indonesian value system.

The Role Played by Food

If you are alert to the sort of entertaining Indonesians typically do, you will notice large buffets that last hours with people coming and going casually, very much like the Open House in the west. While the host desires that the food be tasty and ample, the emphasis of the gathering is emphatically and primarily social. The importance of the event suggests that a meal be served instead of snacks.

When an Indonesian friend hosted a birthday party for his infant son, he invited informally a large number of family and friends. He told us that he was preparing food for 200 and expected people to drop in from 2 p.m. until midnight. When we went in the early evening the food was laid out in an informal buffet and each person helped himself. The meal was fresh, tasty, and served at room temperature. It had been cooked earlier in the day.

This contrasts markedly with the western party meal where a soufflé, a gelatin salad or other tied-to-time items might be featured and control the schedule of events.

BEING ENTERTAINED BY INDONESIANS

Among Indonesians the most common forms of entertainment are to *mampir* (drop in on each other); to have a large group at a sort of open house buffet meal to celebrate a variety of family events; or to entertain a small group of professional colleagues at a restaurant.

Many expatriates have expressed their pleasure at being personal guests in the homes of their Indonesian friends. This is, however, a rare event. Most of the middle-class Indonesians are much more comfortable entertaining in restaurants.

Let's be fair; many Indonesians have small houses and feel they lack room to entertain. Other households may consist of several generations—aged parents, married children and their families and unmarried children. Probably only the husband speaks English well enough to keep a conversation going.

If you are invited 'out' with your counterparts, they will arrange to pick you up. Avoid any effort to pay the bill and never suggest going 'Dutch'. Any gesture made toward picking up the tab is not only poor form, it would offend the Indonesian host.

Demands of the Family

Family obligations almost always take precedence over anything else, including entertaining foreign counterparts. On weekends and public holidays, Indonesians spend their time with their family.

Rites of Hospitality

Sir Stamford Raffles in the 1800s made the following comment about the Javanese. Had he the opportunity to travel throughout the islands, we feel he would have included all Indonesians in his description of the gracious host:

> It is not sufficient that a man should place good food before his guest; he is bound to do more: he should render the meal palatable by kind words and treatment, and soothe him after his journey, and to make his heart glad while he partakes of the refreshment.

Indonesians are generous and gracious hosts; the welfare of the guest is very important. In fact, the arrival of company will stop all planned activity while the guest is greeted and taken care of. The best excuse for being late for an appointment in Indonesia is to say, 'We had a guest.' That explains all tardiness and disturbed plans.

The same obligation for hospitality is part of your servants' ethic, too. You may see them in their quarters having tea with someone who just dropped in while the mop sits in the bucket on the unwashed kitchen floor. Calmly, calmly, *Nyonya*! Having observed the need for hospitality, they will quickly return to their work.

117

How to be a dinner guest is described in 'Entertaining Indonesian Counterparts'. Remember the following:

1. Bring a small gift of flowers, candy or cookies. Your Indonesian hostess would expect the same from her Indonesian guests.

2. Listen for the words of invitation, '*Silakan minum*' or '*Silakan makan*', before drinking or eating.

3. A sip and a nibble are all that are required to be socially correct.

4. Leave something on your plate or you'll be asked to have more.

5. You may be entertained by being shown family photo albums.

6. The children will probably be brought out to meet you and may appear at the end of the evening to shake hands and accompany you to the car.

7. Try to arrive about 10–15 minutes late. That is on time!

8. Check ahead of time to see if your children are included in the invitation. If you ask, the answer will probably be 'Of course.'

A Special Note about Being Entertained

Some ethnic groups, notably the Minahasa, the Bataks and some of the ethnic groups from the 'outer' islands, especially Ambon and Timor, might ask the guest to sing a song or participate in the family entertainment. This would usually occur during the *ramah-tamah* or social time of a welcome or a farewell party.

You have lots of choices. If you know some Indonesian children's or folk songs and are willing to burst into song, do it and be assured that you have won their hearts forever. You can demur and sing a song in your own language; everyone would be thrilled. If you can do simple magic with matchsticks or cards, do that. One westerner has gained local fame with small children by sneezing his false teeth into a handkerchief! If the whole idea of being an entertainer appals you, smile and simply say, 'That's not my *adat* (tradition).'

Your Children's Special Needs

At huge family gatherings, your children may be the object of much attention. Predictable is the query, 'Would you like to stay with us?'

This could fall with joy on the ears of an Indonesian child, secure in his large extended family. It might upset your child who could already be feeling disoriented and insecure in unfamiliar surroundings. At such a time, he does not want to look up and see Mum and Dad smiling broadly at the invitation to stay with someone else. Either talk about this situation ahead of time, or be prepared to interpret it to your child.

Vocabulary

Bebas	When applied to dress, casual, non-specified.
Ramah-tamah	Social time; an informal social meeting. It can also describe a social time before a formal meeting.
Rapat	Usually a meeting, a formal gathering.
Rapi	Neat, orderly (usually refers to dress).

119

MIDDLE-CLASS SOCIAL OBLIGATIONS

Even the most naïve observation about the Indonesian social structure would indicate that it is complex, interdependent and heavy with the sense of obligatory membership in groups—all aimed at promoting the welfare of the community and supporting government policies. The well-meaning expatriate wandering onto the scene and wanting to 'make friends' runs into a series of frustrations. It seems to him that the Indonesians always have time for organised events of any nature but no time for the (western) pleasure of casual friendship.

What follows describes only some of the web of responsibilities and demands on time that pull at most educated and motivated middle-class Indonesians.

They have strong obligations to care for the extended family—in providing education, medical care, emotional support, presence at all the important family parties, etc. This might also include membership just-for-fun in an *arisan*, a social/savings group.

The Bataks and Minahasa have 'clans'; many highly placed Javanese claim membership in a *trah*, based on descent from a common illustrious ancestor. The activities of these ethnic group organisations are similar to the responsibilities of the extended family. There are obligations of membership and cooperation based on one's affiliation with a church, mosque, or temple. This may involve religious education classes, prayer groups, fund-raising groups, choirs, dance troupes, sports teams and sponsorship of the Pramuka, the Indonesian Boy and Girl Scouts.

It is common for businesses to sponsor sports teams. Employees are encouraged to participate. Many businesses organise the wives into groups along the lines of Dharma Wanita (see opposite).

Everyone is enrolled in the Rukun Tetangga, neighbourhood organisations, and expected to respond to their call to clean the roadsides, among other neighbourhood projects. Each household must donate money for a variety of community celebrations, especially those associated with Independence Day on August 17.

Membership in the Korps Pegawai Negri, Indonesian Civil Servants Association, is compulsory for all civil servants and employees of government owned agencies. The Korps Pegawai Negri usually assemble, in *batik* uniforms, in front of their buildings on the 17th of each month.

Dharma Wanita, the organisation for wives of civil servants, is typical of the kind of husband/wife system of social organisation. Membership in this group and others is compulsory and hierarchical. The wife takes the equivalent of her husband's position. Responsibilities are usually very heavy; groups like Dharma Wanita are active in social, educational and community welfare.

The system extends to the highest levels of society. Wives of cabinet ministers have their group, Ibu Ria Pembangunan, which is active in social work.

THE FAMILY BOND

The Indonesian family offers a focus for its members' greatest loyalty, a sustaining system of relationships, and physical and emotional security.

It is a given in Indonesian society that interpersonal relationships are the most important and that each is different. Individuals are aware of their status (and the perquisites or limits of it) and do not normally try to change it. The pattern of the traditional, extended family is supportive (emotionally and economically), safe (you can always go home) and clearly defined. From *bapak*, the most elder male, to the newest infant, they arrange themselves, using words describing age (younger, older) rather than sex (brother, sister).

Parental pressure remains strong for the individual as long as he has a parent living; he asserts similar pressures on his children.

The father or father figure is always held in honour; the wife usually holds the purse-strings and is the object of affection. Where else but in Indonesia would you have this name for a car repair shop: Doa Ibu, a Mother's Prayer?

The Extended Family

The mother-infant bond is reinforced in many ways, from nurse-on-demand comfort at mother's breast to the almost continuous presence of the infant in his mother's arms or in a *slendang*, shoulder sling.

At about age three the child is taught the concept of honour and respect for the father—*asal bapak senang. Bapak* remains a strong but sometimes distant figure in his life. By school age, the child is well integrated into the greater family (and neighbourhood) structure. A bond will usually form between him and an older relative—grandparent, older cousin, aunt or uncle—who will function as a mentor/surrogate parent and often be closer to the child than the blood parent. The emotional base for the child is steadily broadened throughout his childhood with the parents always retaining the position of greatest honour if not always the greatest influence.

In Indonesia, one is considered a child until marriage. Until then, he/she is the responsibility of the parents. An Indonesian who had been educated abroad and living on his own since high school recounted his shock upon returning to Indonesia as an adult and being expected to live with his parents at home. 'Our friends will think that we do not care and are not responsible!' said his anxious parents. Adult 'children' working outside but living at home do not generally retain control of their wages, could have their personal mail opened, are expected to contribute to the costs of educating younger brothers and sisters as well as the support of venerable elders who are not working but living in the house.

Carried to its extreme, this ethic can significantly influence the course of one's life. Observing that a very handsome and capable man was not yet married, even though he was in his mid-thirties, the query was offered, 'Why not?' The answer, given in some detail, made it clear that as the oldest son and the only working member of the family, he was obliged to support his living parents and put his younger brothers through school. When those obligations were met, if he could save enough money to marry, he may. It looked hopeless.

Being loved is synonymous with care, food and physical closeness.

Communal Living

'We share everything,' remarked a good friend. In fact, this sense of common ownership and the right to take and use makes it very difficult for the Indonesian to accumulate capital (savings). If a person has squirrelled aside a bit of savings and some close friend or family member knows about it, he may express a need for—and expect to receive it.

The physical need to return to the family is most obvious to the foreigner at the holiday of Lebaran when the cities empty and everyone who can, goes home. The professional beggars join this exodus. A sociologist was quoted as remarking, 'Among relatives in the village, they'll patch up the psychological blows they endure in the city. They long for the healing of the *kampung* (village).' The fact that they will probably lie about their lives in the city is missing the point; they return to the village with the money they have saved and celebrate in a large familial orgy of gift-giving and spending.

The sense of shared feelings and responsibility for action causes the Indonesian to think first of the society as a whole. He experiences shame if his conduct deviates from the group norm. This contrasts sharply with the stress on individuality in the west and the resultant feelings of guilt if one's performance is inferior.

'In personal relations, we tend to think that if you don't know your second cousin, you're not civilised, you have no warmth in you,' said one Indonesian woman whose parents' home holds about 20 people.

Westerners have discovered, when giving friends and colleagues a ride home after work that 'home' may change frequently from the residence of an aunt to that of an older brother or a cousin's husband. Yet each is 'home' and the individual feels a legitimate claim to it. Rarely will a person feel he has no place.

Life in an Indonesian family was characterised by a young woman as '… not particularly active, or conducive to productivity. On the other hand, no one is sent to an old age home.'

THE ARISAN

Throughout the islands there exist social/savings groups, usually of women, called *arisan*. These groups can comprise members of an extended family, employees of a company, neighbours—in fact, any social group. They usually meet once a month for a special meal and to put an agreed amount of money into the 'pot'.

The amount can range from Rp. 1000 to Rp. 1,000,000. A name is drawn for the month's winner. The *arisan* exists until each person has 'won'. If you get the money first, it is like a loan; if you get it last, it's savings! Then the *arisan* reorganises and begins again.

The *arisan* also engages in cooperative buying of large appliances refrigerators, sewing machines—sets of dishes or even gold. Because they buy in bulk, each *arisan* member receives high quality goods at below market prices.

THE COCKTAIL PARTY

The typical western cocktail party is not a normal social setting for most Indonesians for the following reasons: they do not drink alcohol; there is a strong ethic to keep business in the office and not in one's home or as part of the entertainment; and most Indonesians prefer to socialise in specified groups, i.e., of family members, women's auxiliaries, *arisan* (mutual savings groups), school or religious groups. Therefore, the idea of men and women gathering in a quasi-business setting where refreshments always include alcohol is uncommon in their culture, and lacking clear clues for comfortable behaviour.

In addition, Indonesians do not like to stand and eat. Their attitude is aptly stated: '*Makannya seperti kuda*, Horses eat standing!'

The women, especially young wives in the developing middle class, tell us they are ill at ease about their skill with the language and their ability to initiate a conversation.

HOLIDAYS

The Department of Religious Affairs of the Republic of Indonesia fixes the official public holidays each year. The ones below are official for government offices and schools. The dates of Muslim holidays slip annually by 11 days because of the use of the 29/30-day lunar calendar. The holidays that are usually also observed in the business community are indicated.

Tahun Baru (New Year's Day)

January 1 is celebrated here as in the west. Businesses are closed.

Nyepi (Hindu New Year)

This most energetically celebrated holiday in Bali occurs at the spring equinox. The celebration is really a study in contrasts.

The day before the new year there is a general cleaning of the villages, a frantic cooking of food for gods and man, ceremonial (but real) cockfights and a noisy night-time bit of yelling and parading and driving out of devils. It is believed that then the Lord of Hell, Yama, sweeps Hades of devils which fall on Bali, and the whole of the island must be purified.

The following day, Nyepi, is supposed to be utterly still and without human activity. Roads are deserted, villages quiet, shops closed and tourists with a short time on the island frustrated.

Wafat Isa Almasih (Good Friday)

This is observed in the traditional manner by Christian groups. Muslims honour Jesus as a prophet. General business is not significantly affected.

Isra Mi'raj Nabi Muhammad (Night of the Ascent)

This Muslim holiday commemorates the night in the tenth year of Muhammad's prophethood when the Archangel Gabriel conducted him through the seven heavens, where he spoke with God, and from which he returned the same night with instructions that included the institution in Islam of the five daily prayers. General business is not significantly affected.

Kenaikan Isa Almasih (Ascension of Christ)

This day is observed by Christians throughout the islands. It is not a holiday for most businessmen.

Waisak (Vesak Day)

The anniversary of Buddha's reaching Nirvana. Buddhists come from far to celebrate this day at the Borobudur monument in Central Java, one of the architectural wonders of the Buddhist world, ranking along with the temple complex of Angkor Wat in Cambodia and Pagan in Burma. General business is not affected.

Idul Fitri—Lebaran (End of Fast of Ramadan)

Throughout the islands the expatriate will note at least three visible (and audible) manifestations of the celebrations of Lebaran. First, several days before the holiday, the streets will fill with people selling *ketupat*, small woven palm-leaf containers in which rice is steamed and made ready for feeding visitors. Second, at sundown on the last day of fasting, the roadways fill with young people in trucks, on bikes or on foot, yelling and beating drums in the *takbir*, a prayer on Idul Fitri eve. Third, on the first day of Idul Fitri, the visiting begins. During the two days of Lebaran, 'inferiors' go to the homes of their 'superiors', young people call on their elders and government dignitaries hold open house.

Families go out on motorbikes, in buses and cars, and entire *kampungs* load into large trucks. They meet to ask forgiveness for past mistakes and faults, '*Selamat Idul Fitri: Ma'afkan Lahir Batin*' (Happy Lebaran and may you forgive all our wrongs and unexpressed hostile sentiments!)

Significance of Lebaran for the Expatriate: Muslims observe the fasting regulations (*puasa*) during Ramadan and will not eat from before dawn until after sunset to emphasise spiritual values and discipline.

The expatriate will quickly realise how profoundly this exercise affects business and social life for the month. Those fasting tire early and easily; efficiency is lowered and patience wears thin; the heat serves to increase fatigue. Social demands within the Muslim world are heavy—to pray, and to break the fast in great social groups. Gastric illnesses are more common as the belly is alternately empty and hungry and then packed with food.

The sensitive employer will not eat too lustily in the presence of fasting servants and remember that the day is very long for those who observe all the religious obligations. Be prepared also for employees needing extra money (usually in the form of a bonus of a month's salary) for the gifts that must be purchased at this time, the new clothes, special foods, and additionally, time off to return to the *kampungs* for celebrations with their families there.

Send Lebaran cards to your Muslim friends and pay social calls if you want to participate in the spirit of the holiday. Many foreigners have found that a gift of homemade cookies or cakes is welcomed.

During this time many shops either shut down completely for several days or weeks or work at half staff strength to allow their employees time to return to the *kampungs.*

Proklamasi Kemerdekaan Republik Indonesia (Independence Day, August 17)

This significant day is celebrated nationally. The expatriate will probably be asked to contribute money to the neighbourhood celebrations. He may also display the Indonesian flag at his residence and attach a small one to his car; the streets sprout flag sellers at this time. Most business places close for this holiday; some observe special, shortened hours.

Idul Adha (Festival of the Sacrifice)

Also known as Idul Korban and Lebaran Haji, this holiday acknowledges three significant aspects of Islam. First, the date coincides with the time that the faithful in Mecca begin their pilgrimage around the *kaabah*; second, the act of sacrificing animals commemorates the willingness of Abraham to sacrifice his son Ishmael; third, in Indonesia it is a time to visit the burial grounds, clean the graves and decorate them with flowers. Some women bring food to the graveyard to give to the poor.

The expatriate will notice immediately the great number of animals on sale for slaughter at this time. Every grass verge seems to be growing goats; cattle are tethered beneath trees. Animals purchased by individuals or families are given to the mosques where the Committee of Sacrifice (Panitia Korban) handles the slaughter and distribution of meat to the poor. Most businesses are closed at this time.

Tahun Baru Hijriyah (Hegira, Islamic New Year)

This holiday celebrates the very first day of the Muslim era in AD 622 when Muhammad left Mecca to start a new community in Medina. The H after the years in the Muslim era means 'after the Hijriyah or Hegira'; thus 1406H is understood as one thousand, four hundred and six years by the Islamic calendar since the migration.

Maulid Nabi Muhammad
(Prophet Muhammad's Birthday)

Muslims honour Muhammad as the last in the line of prophets that includes Noah, Moses, David, John the Baptist and Jesus. Muslims believe that through Muhammad God delivered or revealed a perfect message and this is recorded in the Koran.

The commemoration of Muhammad's birthday begins on the 12th day of the third month (Rabiul Awal) and lasts a month with *selamatans* (special prayer ceremonies) in homes, mosques and

129

schools. During this time the youth groups are active doing social work in the community.

Natal Hari Pertama (Christmas Day)

This is celebrated by Christians in the traditional manner. Business places are closed.

Imlek (Chinese New Year)

Though not an official holiday, it is widely celebrated in varying degrees throughout the island. The first thing the expatriate notices is that the prices of oranges and other symbolic fruits will rise; the second is that the stores that are closed for the holiday are a measure of the businesses owned by the Indonesian Chinese. Almost all these stores will close for two days and many for a week or more.

Within the Chinese community, there is social gambling and the eating of special foods, among them noodles for long life and oranges for good luck. Younger family members visit the elders to pay respects. Children get *hongbao*, red packets with money in even amounts. By tradition, new clothes must be acquired; the floor is not swept on the first day (this would sweep away good luck); and all persons try to finish their business and meet their obligations before the year ends.

The expatriate wishing to participate may do so by sending cards or gifts of fruit to Chinese friends. These would say *Selamat Tahun Baru* or *Gong Xi Fa Cai*—both of which mean Happy New Year!

ISLAM

Most expatriates in Indonesia will observe rather than participate in Islamic life. Therefore we include this discussion of Islam in Indonesia as a social event from the foreign point of view. In fact, for many Indonesians, their activities associated with Islam are synonymous with their social life.

One of the most obvious manifestations of Islam are the vast crowds of men streaming to mosques every Friday for prayers, some clad in *sarungs* and shirts, others in white garments brought back from the *haj* or pilgrimage. Schoolchildren from Islamic schools fill the roads, the little girls with their heads and necks covered in accordance with Islamic rules of feminine modesty. Pork is always sold just outside the municipal meat markets, out of deference to Muslim dietary restrictions. Some servants refuse to work in a house which has dogs. There are exuberant holidays, usually marked by the slaughter of animals. And there is the early morning amplified call to prayer, which alerts the neighbourhood to the new day.

Sunlight flashes from the shiny metal roofs of mosques the length of the archipelago. Indonesia has the largest Islamic population in the world. However, the government emphasises that, in the spirit of *Pancasila*, each person is free to practise the religion of his choice. There is no state religion.

Islam in Indonesia

Islam arrived in the trading ports of North Sumatra in the early 1500s with Arabic and Indian Muslim traders and teachers. Second strongholds were established in southern Sulawesi and the north coast of Java in the 1600s. The history of Islam encountering the native religions is not so much one of confrontation as of accommodation and absorption. The attitude is maintained today and accounts, in part, for the variations in Islamic practices observed throughout Indonesia.

Effects of Islam on the Arts

Islam modified, but did not change, the basic art forms of the islands. Muslim prohibition of the realistic portrayal of human or animal figures is reflected in many of the stylised *batik* patterns. (*Batik* from areas of minimal Islamic influence is alive with animal and human forms.) Only in the *wayang kulit*, Javanese shadow puppetry, are the human shapes retained.

131

The dynamic dance styles of India were modified for modesty into the highly disciplined and restrained dances seen in Central Java today, and many of the early mosques show a combination of Hindu and Islamic architecture.

The Islamic Year

The Islamic lunar calendar is only one of several calendars used. Dates for the holy days are announced by Islamic officials.

Islamic Presence Today

Throughout Indonesia, the mosques are centres for social, educational and spiritual activities. They sponsor sports teams and urge youth groups to make collections for various social causes, organise religious activities for the entire family and maintain schools.

For the expatriate, the amplified call to prayer at about 4:30 in the morning will be his first encounter with Islam. It comes with the assurance that prayer is better than sleep.

The Koran mentions three obligatory prayers a day, but tradition indicates five; the first is at sunset, followed by those at night, dawn, noon and afternoon. Dawn is a bit of a misnomer. There is a widely known folk guide in Indonesia for determining the 'correct' time for the dawn prayer. If a person can tell the difference between a white and a black thread viewed in natural light, it is too late!

Keeping Religious Obligations

The five principles of Islam are: the confession of faith, the performance of the ritual prayer five times a day, the payment of the religious tax, observing the fast of Ramadan, and performing the pilgrimage to Mecca (the *haj*).

Preparing for Prayer

Before prayer, purification rites must be performed in the following order to establish purity of intention: using the *air wudu* (ordinary water), the Muslim must wash hands from the wrist down, three times; gargle and spit to cleanse the mouth; wash the face; wash both hands up to the elbows; moisten part of the head, comb the hair with water; and wash both feet up to the ankles.

A man must present himself for prayer pure in person and thought. If anything happens to change this state—being touched by a dog, a woman, going to the bathroom, passing intestinal gas—he is obliged to repeat the ritual purification.

Appropriate Dress for Prayer

Muslim women at prayer wear the *mukena* which covers most of the body. The men wear the *kain sarung* and a plain shirt. They are often seen walking to the mosque carrying the *sejadah* (prayer rug).

Making a Place for Prayer

Most commercial and office buildings have a *musholla*, a place for prayer. Men generally pray at the mosque, women traditionally pray in their homes.

A concerned citizen in Java made a request in a local newspaper that the state-owned railway company, the PJKA, provide at least one *musholla* on the trains. It is impossible for practising Muslims to pray in the station for fear of missing their train, he stated.

Living Under Islamic Law

Some actions under Islamic law may be described as:

Halal	Permissible, neither rewarded nor punished.
Haram	Forbidden.
Makruh	Undesirable, rewarded for not doing, unpunished for doing.
Sunah	Desirable, rewarded for doing, unpunished for omitting.
Wajib	Obligatory, rewarded for doing, punished for omitting.

Dietary Restrictions

Islam prohibits the use of alcoholic beverages and the eating of pork. There are other food prohibitions which pertain only to certain parts of the country. When entertaining, it is always best to find out what is correct in your area.

Marriage and Divorce

Islam tradition permits a man up to four wives and many of the older Indonesian Muslims, especially in the rural areas, do have several wives concurrently. The marriage law, P.P.10, enacted in 1974, provides national legislation to protect the rights of women and it is the official policy to keep families together. In practice, couples can, within the law, dissolve the marriage contract.

Do/Taboo in a Mosque

Visitors are generally welcome in the mosques. They should observe the following rules:

- If in doubt, ask permission to enter.
- Remove shoes before entering. It helps to wear shoes that can be removed easily.
- Observe quiet and respectful behaviour.
- Walk behind persons who are praying.
- Dress modestly; women wear garments with long sleeves and men wear long trousers.
- Ask permission before taking photographs.
- Be careful not to touch any person or object, especially the Holy Koran.
- Women who are menstruating may not enter a mosque.

Vocabulary

Air wudu	Water used to wash parts of the body before prayer.
Azan	The call to prayer.

Masjid	Enclosure for prayer. Depending on your area of Indonesia, it will be called:
masigit	Sunda (West Java)
mesigi	Sulawesi
mesigit	Java
meuseugit	Acheh
Masjid jami	Mosque used for Friday prayer, also known as the Friday mosque. Smaller prayer houses used for single prayers and not for prayer meetings are called:
langgar	Java
langgara	Sulawesi
meunasah	Acheh
surau	West Sumatra
Minaret (*menara*)	The tower usually found just outside the mosque.
Muezzin	The man who traditionally called the faithful to prayer five times a day. Now this function is given to cassettes and electrical amplification.
Musholla (mushalla)	Prayer house not routinely used for Friday meetings.
Sejadah	Prayer rug.

Words to Say

As salaamu 'alaikum	Islamic greeting: 'Peace be with you.'
Alaikum salaam	'And upon you, peace'—the correct response to the above.

SELAMATAN

This is one of the ceremonies that foreigners are quick to hear of, possibly may never attend, and usually have some misconceptions about. The word means 'a religious meal' and that is exactly what it is. It is emphatically not a party in the generally understood sense.

A *selamatan* can be given in any situation that one wants to be special. Its intent is to secure good fortune and harmony for those involved. There will always be elders or officials who will say the prayers and then a meal that is shared with those present and often sent around to neighbours or concerned friends.

One may have a *selamatan* when the roof is raised on a new house, when a major journey is undertaken, when a situation is deemed intolerable and out of harmony—or for any of a number of reasons.

Westerners living in Indonesia have had *selamatans* to open a meeting house, to change 'bad vibes' at a place of work, to seek to stop a rash of accidents in the home, to bless a home that was being lived in for the first time by foreigners, and to ask for calm to be restored after the death of a treasured pet. In every case, the arrangements were made by trusted Indonesian friends to honour the traditional intent of the ritual.

Chapter Seven

THE LIFE CIRCLE

Each Indonesian is heir to the traditions of his *suku* (ethnic group) and the rituals of his religion. Together they form customs of richness and depth that surround all aspects of an individual's cosmic circle —birth, adolescence, marriage and death.

In this chapter, we explain the sequence of events at these occasions, giving tips on correct behaviour, words to say, and suggestions for gifts. We do not focus in depth on ethnic detail for the following reasons: there are far too many to include; many of the ceremonies considered most traditional are as practised in the royal families and not by the majority of the people; and we wanted the information to be broad enough to encourage the expatriate to discover some of the details with his host.

The elite and noble families, some of whom retain feudal responsibilities, are generally acknowledged to be *adat yang betul* (truly traditional). Other families are said to be *adat di adatkan* (observing *adat* for the status of the family). Not every Indonesian chooses to observe all the traditions nor can he afford to. Human nature being what it is, individuals pick from this rich treasury ceremonies to meet their needs, means and interest.

In collecting data that would reflect the contemporary practice of traditional behaviour, we encountered:

- a vast amount of detailed, dated (most before 1950), and technical, anthropological and linguistic research material;
- young (under 50) Indonesians who needed to confer with elders to get details of ceremonies because, they said, 'We don't really do all of that anymore'; and
- many not able to provide information about ethnic groups other than their own.

In pursuing his own inquiries, the expatriate may find that only within the last 25 years have Indonesians been able to travel easily throughout the archipelago and to become familiar with other cultures. With the assistance of the cultural programming on television (TVRI) and culture parks like Taman Mini Indonesia Indah near Jakarta, the First Lady, Madam Ibu Tien Suharto, and others have suggested that Indonesians can develop a wider appreciation of the nation's cultural heritage.

This chapter contains examples of ceremonies associated with birth, babies and circumcision. In 'Marriage—the Grand Moment', we touch briefly on the pre-nuptial ceremonies and then move to the reception and the importance of that grand party. 'Death—the Islamic Community' and 'Death—the Chinese Community' describe the sequence of events and proper behaviour for the family of the deceased and those who *melawat* (pay condolence calls). 'Caring for the Spirits' explains the varying attitudes toward visiting and tending the graves.

Finally, our friends tell us that the best social advice is to watch the group and do what they do. Indonesians are gracious hosts and eager to include guests in special events. If your host is Batak, count on him to explain the symbolism of the ceremonies; a Javanese, Balinese or Minahasa would graciously do the same.

Therefore, wherever you find yourself, if you are invited to participate in the special 'cosmic' ceremonies of your neighbours and friends, do so.

BIRTHS AND BABIES

Babies are wanted, treasured and guarded against all manner of evil. It is fact not folklore that infant mortality is still very high in Indonesia, especially in the provinces. The most poignant reminder of how temporary life is for some are the rows and rows of tiny graves that dimple the *kampung* graveyards. Rare is the villager who has not buried many of his children.

Parents zealously use all means to protect their babies through the fragile first five years. Some newborns are given the juice of turmeric, believed to guarantee a healthy child with a strong stomach impervious to intestinal worms. Others are given honey for the same reason.

On Java, some village children wear threads, *lawe*, and amulets around their necks or waists. These strings of handspun cotton are placed on the child by the mother, grandmother or the *dukun* (native medicine practitioner), and said to have the power to protect the child from evil, illness and early death.

The official response to the problem of childhood mortality is to establish 'well-baby clinics' (*Anak-anak Balita*, literally, 'children below the age of five'). These are spreading education and medical assistance throughout the provinces.

Babies are cherished and welcomed into the family. Rarely is a small child far from the security of someone's lap or arms.

Welcoming Ceremonies

Almost all ceremonies for newborns combine the sense of welcome to the community with prayers for strength and good health. These vary with the ethnic group and within social levels.

Among the Bataks, when a child is seven days old, the mother pounds a rice cake with sugar and spices and takes it into the *kampung* to offer to the villagers and to 'show the baby the sun' for the first time. A more elaborate variation of the same ceremony involves a lengthy procession of villagers who, in prayer and ritual, introduce the child to the village and the village spirits and bathe him in the *pemandian* (bathing area). A feast is prepared and the special food—a fish—is touched to the lips of the baby with the wish that the spirit keepers of the village will guard him.

When a Minangkabau girl is born into a noble family, her maternal grandfather will bring gold bracelets, and add a name for the child; her paternal grandparents give her a milk-cow calf (*anak sapi*). In a family of commoners, the gift would be a live chicken.

Christian families would have a baptism followed by a large meal for all the guests.

Tujuh Bulan for Mother, Turun Tanah for Baby

Two ceremonies are observed widely in varying forms: the *tujuh bulan* ritual bathing of the mother-to-be and the *turun tanah* ceremony for the infant. These ceremonies are an eclectic mixture of animist practices, folklore and, among some groups, prayers. However analysed, they surely typify the syncretic nature of many rituals.

Western baby showers and parties with gifts for the mother-to-be are not traditional in Indonesia. It is considered incautious and presumptuous to celebrate too much before the event.

In Bali the bathing ceremony is done at the third month; most other groups observe the *tujuh bulan* (seventh month) *selamatan*. The Toba Bataks have a ceremony called *tujuh bulan* but it is a feast with *ikan mas* (carp) and prayers, and no ritual bath.

141

Generally, it is a time of supplication for good health for all and the mother-to-be is given a great deal of emotional support from other women with living children. Various rituals involve special flowers, fruit, scented or blessed water, cloth and food.

The Javanese and Sundanese, in addition to the bath, have a *selamatan* with a delightful ceremony: the mother-to-be 'sells' *rojak* (a super spicy fruit salad) and *cendol* (drink) to the guests who use pieces of clay roof tile as currency. The spontaneous comments of the guests regarding the taste of the *rojak* is thought by some to indicate the sex or describe the personality of the child. It is also hoped that this act of commerce will encourage thrift in the child!

The ceremony of *turun tanah* or introducing the child to the earth (where he will spend the rest of his life) is considered to have very ancient origins and is common—with various ethnic nuances throughout the islands. In Bali the ceremony is performed after 210 days. The child is officially welcomed to the family, his hair is cut, and efforts are made to read his future. Among the Minangkabau the ceremony is also called *turun mandi*. It is primarily a ceremony to cut the hair of the child to encourage physical strength and growth.

The Javanese make a large party of it. Special objects—gold items, a pen, a book, and more—are strewn about an enclosed area. Anticipation runs high to see which object will attract the child's attention and thus illuminate aspects of his future.

Some noble and traditional families on Java place the child on seven *kain batik* (lengths of *batik* cloth) that his mother wore at her *tujuh bulan* ceremony. These may be kept for the life of the individual. The fabrics that clothed the mother before the birth are used for the *turun tanah* of her child and then again to wrap the body at death.

Advice to the Expatriate

Many of these ceremonies—on Java—are patterned after the behaviour and ritual of the nobles and royalty in the courts at Yogyakarta and Surakarta. Many modern upper class families enjoy the parties, gift-giving and socialising. In the small rural villages, the rituals are as enjoyable but less elaborate. If you are invited to a *turun tanah* ceremony of a friend's child, a gift of clothing or toys would be appreciated.

Visiting New Babies

In many groups—Javanese, Sundanese, Minangkabau, Batak and Balinese, for example—it is common for the new mother to rest for the first month to 40 days. (Many modern mothers will begin to socialise on a limited scale in this time.)

When the mother and child are ready to receive visitors, call with a wrapped gift. If the mother and baby are Chinese, visitors are welcome anytime. Chinese families will cut the baby's hair for the first time at 40 days. They prepare a special meal of chicken and dyed red eggs which they send to relatives and close friends. This is also one of the ways they will acknowledge gifts sent to the baby at his birth. Standard baby gifts are acceptable: clothing or a fork, spoon or baby cup in silver. The quality of the relationship/friendship between the families is reflected in the quality of the gift.

In the cities, acknowledge the birth with a gift of flowers sent to the maternity home as soon as you know mother and baby are well. Both husband and wife would sign the card. Increasingly, in the larger cities, the parents will respond with a thank you card, giving the child's name.

Do/Taboo

- Proper etiquette suggests that a gift worth Rp. 5000 has more emotional value to the recipient than a cash gift of Rp. 10,000.
- Sometimes one sees baby manicure sets. Avoid giving as gifts those with scissors or other sharp-pointed objects.
- Say '*Selamat datang kelahiran putri/putra*' (Best wishes on the birth of your daughter/son) on the card.

CIRCUMCISION

Circumcision or *sunatan*, an important event in the life of a young Muslim male, marks his passage from childhood to adulthood, and is usually observed between the ages of 11 and 12. This rite is regarded as *sunah* or optional in Islam.

In times past, the circumcision was a public event. Now, in urban areas it is a medical procedure with appropriate facilities and treatment. However, even today in the very rural and isolated areas in Java, young boys are awakened before dawn on the morning of their circumcision and taken to a cold mountain stream. There they immerse themselves until the icy water has produced a state of general anaesthetic to dull the pain of the procedure.

Generally throughout Indonesia, several days after the circumcision, the family holds a party to which expatriate friends might be

Public benefactors regularly sponsor mass circumcision ceremonies for the sons of those who cannot afford to have it done.

invited. As in most Indonesian social moments, it is a time of sharing festive foods and light drinks with family and friends. At the circumcision celebration party a gift of money, Rp. 10,000–15,000, in a plain white envelope, is given to the boy.

In the past, it was common for families to lavish vast amounts of money at these parties, dressing the boys in elegant costumes and staging elaborate parties involving the entire neighbourhood. Today, in East Java the young men are attired as princes and carried on beautifully caparisoned horses that dance and prance their way through the village. In other areas the boys 'ride' hobby horses held on the shoulders of friends. In still other areas, the boys are moved through the streets in decorated *becaks* or other forms of transport.

Unless they are very close friends of the family, foreigners are not usually included in these ceremonies. However, many appreciate and own hand-carved copies of the low, wide circumcision chair used as a seat of honour by males in the noble families associated with the Kraton (the palace of Javanese nobles of Surakarta or Yogyakarta).

Words to Say

At the party the guests are expected to give a blessing to the young man. The following statements are appropriate.

Selamat	May you be blessed.
Selamat atas khitanan adik	Congratulations on the occasion of your circumcision.
Semoga adik menjadi anak yang baik.	We hope you grow up to be a good boy.

MARRIAGE—THE GRAND MOMENT

Within the Indonesian culture, with the exception of the Hindu Balinese, marriage is the most significant life cycle experience for a woman. It indicates a completeness in her life—the end of

145

childhood, the achievement of adulthood, the binding together of the couple and their families, the promise of children.

'Well, of course it is expected that everyone will marry,' explained one middle-aged unmarried Indonesian professional woman. 'It is most important that one remain open to the possibility of marriage.' Other friends added anecdotes that emphasised the importance of marriage—even if brief or tragic. Such a marriage is not half so tragic in the eyes of most Indonesians as never having wed.

This chapter does not explain marriage ceremonies in ethnic detail. Rather we would emphasise that within the broad framework of Islam or Christianity, the proper behaviour of the guest is the same—polite and respectful, unobtrusive yet aware of what others are doing.

Expatriates routinely notice three major differences between the marriage ceremonies in the west and in Indonesia:
- The pre-nuptial ceremonies that occur over a period of time preceding the wedding usually involve a lavish exchange of gifts between not only the principals but also the two families.
- The costumes of the ethnic groups that are usually splendid.
- The need to host the most lavish possible wedding reception.

Pre-nuptial Ceremonies

Engagements can be long here: students will complete their studies; some must resolve family commitments; others need time to accumulate money for the festivities.

During this time, there are numerous ceremonies of varying degrees of formality featuring the exchange of gifts, money, gold, fruit and flowers—often embellished by rituals. The intent is to bind the families and the couple, to establish the quality of personal relationship so important to Indonesians.

There can be a marvellous mix of contemporary prayers with *adat* and animist traditions. Many friends remarked that they could not separate religion from tradition in some ceremonies. The Javanese and Sundanese, for example, have a ritual bathing of the bride-to-be (and sometimes the groom-to-be), accompanied by prayers and assisted by family members. Another custom has some of the ritual decorations or materials placed at the crossroads, signifying that there shall be no end to the relationship and their happiness.

Most of these ceremonies seek to achieve harmony, prosperity and longevity for the couple. While in olden times there were carefully established traditions for these events, now they seem to be observed for the memorable pleasure of embellishment.

When foreigners express interest in these customs, they are almost always invited to observe them.

Wedding Costumes and Paraphernalia

A most popular ladies' entertainment is the staging of traditional ethnic wedding costumes from throughout Indonesia. Everyone loves the lavish spectacle!

'Traditional' for many Chinese, Betawi (native Jakartans) and Minahasa brides means the flowing white lace and tulle of the western wedding gown. This is either rented or kept in the family and used by succeeding generations of brides.

The traditional Javanese wear fitted black velvet jackets and fine *tulis* (hand-drawn) *kain batik panjang*. Sundanese brides wear the *kain batik* but substitute a fine white *kebaya* (blouse) for the velvet jacket. Batak brides will receive many special *ulos* (woven scarves usually placed around the shoulders). Minangkabau brides are colourful in their ornate gold headdresses and displays of worked gold on their red or bright blue costumes.

Furnishings for the wedding reception usually involve creating the impression of the couple enthroned. Most hotels can provide the elaborate furniture needed by the principals. There are business houses that rent the full kit—costumes for different ethnic groups and all the furniture, lights and accessories.

It is common now for a family to hire the services of a lady to

The beauty and ceremony of the traditional Javanese wedding is familiar and appreciated by all.

arrange and manage the wedding—select the ceremonies to be observed, see to the catering, coach the family in their roles, arrange a timetable of events, attend to the bride's make-up and costume, and arrange for photographers and videotaping. Special bridal beauty shops may provide similar services.

The Akad Nikah (Legal Ceremony)

The *akad nikah*, held to satisfy religious and civil law for all Muslim ethnic groups, is a gathering of the closest family. It does not have the broader emotional and social significance of the reception.

Invitations for the *akad nikah* and the reception are generally sent out together. The wording of an invitation to the reception makes it clear that one's presence at the reception is perceived as bringing a blessing to the young couple.

The Reception

A small family wedding would number several hundred here. The typical reception draws several thousand from all over the islands.

A friend said, 'The reception is the family's announcement that the marriage has occurred; all who come bring blessings to the couple, so naturally we want everyone to be there.' 'We invite everyone we know and then multiply by three!' added a Muslim Sundanese friend. A Chinese Christian friend recounted that she always invites interested foreigners. 'Come along to the reception with me. There will be a huge crowd. You have never seen anything like it. They will be delighted if you come.' All of that is true!

Families will go into debt, sell livestock and land to raise money for the reception. The Minangkabau have an idiom which describes the need to obtain funds for the reception: '*Kalau tidak ada kayu, jenjang dikeping.*' If there is no wood, cut the ladder (to the house).

Events at the Reception

The Chinese usually hold the reception in a restaurant or hotel. There will be table seating; if the party is too large, there may be a wedding buffet similar to that described here. If the setting allows, the groom and the father of the bride will move from table to table exchanging toasts with the guests.

The sequence of events at most wedding receptions is simple. Sign the guest book, leave your gift, greet the bridal party in the reception line, help yourself to the wedding buffet, say your goodbyes and leave—in that order.

Sometimes the reception is so large that the hall (*gedung pertamuan*) so crowded, it is possible to stand in line for up to an hour and not see anyone you know. A western couple at one such large reception left their gift, entered the hall and finally glimpsed the wedding couple from afar. Horrors! Wrong wedding party! They reclaimed their gift with a smile and hastened to the right one.

As the evening begins, the wedding party will gather and make

149

its way to the decorated dais. There is usually an announcer who makes remarks no one appears to listen to and the bride's and groom's families may offer *sambutans*, speeches of praise. If the couple is Christian, there may be a prayer. The invitation to eat, '*Silakan makan*,' will be given and at the same time the receiving line will begin to form.

The formal receiving line is so common here that rarely will you see the bridal pair mix with the guests and never will you see them make a token appearance and then leave.

If you know the bridal couple, offer the traditional wedding wishes in the language you normally use. If you do not know them well, smile and say '*Selamat berbahagia*' (Best wishes). Inspired conversation is not necessary! Having made your greetings, move to the wedding buffet, help yourself to the food, then find a chair and eat. At the buffet table and around the chairs, waiters circulate to remove dirty dishes placed on the floor or given to them. The role of the guest is entirely passive. Once you have eaten, you may wish to stay and socialise. Remember though that these parties can be very crowded and not all the reception halls are airconditioned.

To be absolutely correct, one should go through the reception line twice. When you greet the wedding couple with your formal words, 'Congratulations' or '*Selamat berbahagia*,' the couple's reply of '*Terima kasih*' is thanking you for your blessing. When you go through the line again prior to departure and once again repeat the formal words or ask permission to leave, '*Permisi*,' the couple's response of '*Terima kasih*' is now thanking you for your gift, your attention, and your presence there!

Correct Wedding Gifts

Upper class: Gifts for this group must be obviously expensive: a television set, gas cooker, or piece of furniture. Equally acceptable are luxury items such as crystal, an electrical appliance, or silver. Avoid handicrafts and casual *batik* goods (placemats, napkins, etc.).

As individuals can rarely afford such expense, most offices have a collection, called *patokan* or *iuran*. Office employees contribute regularly to this to create a fund which is used to purchase gifts for weddings, births and other occasions. Names of all participants in the collection group are put on the card attached to the gift. It is a sensitive way to satisfy the outward appearance of great expense without financial stress to the giver. As a foreigner, you may participate in this arrangement in the office.

Middle class: Correct gifts are a set of dishes, glassware, an electrical appliance, an object for the home that is visible (an ornament rather than a bathtowel), or a full tablecloth if it is imported and expensive. Avoid towels and sheets unless these are 'fancy' and imported. If the couple is Chinese and from a moderate background, it is acceptable to give a generous gift of money in a red packet (*hongbao*).

Kampung: Appropriate gifts are a set of serving dishes, a length of good quality *batik*, 2–3 metres of good cloth, sheets, pots and pans, or decorative glass objects. Gold, such as a small ring, is also acceptable, if it is to your servant. Avoid giving food or towels.

It is sometimes difficult for the expatriate to appreciate how honoured people are that you have accepted their invitation. They enjoy the opportunity to be the host. If you take pictures, it is thoughtful to send copies of photos, or if you wish to pursue it, to drop in and deliver them yourself!

Wedding Thank You Notes

Twenty-five years ago, Indonesian brides penned personal thank you notes to the reception guests and usually followed that with a social call. Those exquisite manners have gone the way of modernity.

Today, as you sign the guest register and hand over the gift, attendants give you a card that thanks you for coming and for your attention. It is also the thank you card for the gift.

Dressing Correctly

Upper-class wedding reception: A man is expected to wear a western business suit. Women should choose a plain classic garment in an obviously fine fabric with sleeves or a jacket.

Middle-class wedding reception: If the invitation says lounge suit, the man is expected to wear a western business suit. If dress is not specified, a long-sleeved *batik* shirt and dark trousers are correct. A woman should wear a nice afternoon dress in subdued colours with sleeves or a jacket.

***Kampung* wedding reception:** These are the social events for your servants and possibly some of your neighbours if you live near a *kampung*. A man should wear a long-sleeved *batik* shirt and dark trousers, women in a nice cotton day dress or a good skirt and blouse. Children should wear their 'best', including shoes and socks.

You may see very extravagant costumes on your Indonesian hosts in a style called *kampungan*, which means a little extreme and unsophisticated. The children could be decked out in rhinestone jewellery, dressed with an abundance of rayon ribbon, flounces and ruffles. High fashion for a male guest could be a new pair of blue jeans. Reflect that for many people of this class, the wedding represents an opportunity to buy new clothes.

Do/Taboo

- At all social levels the wedding reception is the major ceremony. Your presence is perceived as a blessing and appreciated.
- Dress appropriately.
- Gifts of money are inappropriate to your social equals.

Vocabulary

Akad nikah	The legal wedding ceremony.
Bernikah	To wed. Don't confuse this with the colloquail *kahwin* (mate or breed).
Selamat berbahagia	Best wishes.

Words to Say (on cards)

If you are unable to attend the reception but wish to acknowledge the invitation with a gift, send it addressed to both bride and groom to her home with a card: '*Selamat dan bahagia atas pernikahan anda berdua.*' (Best wishes to both of you on your wedding.)

If you wish to acknowledge the invitation, but not with a major gift, send a small bouquet of flowers to the home of the bride a day or so before the ceremonies with a note: '*Selamat berbahagia.*' (Best wishes.)

A statement that you are unable to attend is: '*Terima kasih atas undangan pernikahan putra/putri Bapak dan Ibu, tetapi sayang kami berhalangan untuk hadir. Semoga kedua mempelai sangat berbahagia.*' (Thank you for the invitation to the wedding. We regret that we will be unable to attend. Best wishes to the couple.)

DEATH

The foreigner is quick to observe the yellow paper flags tied on trees and poles along a street that announce a death in the community. Cars and crowds fill the way. Police direct traffic or close the road. Someone has died and the family and friends are gathering.

Of all the traditional life events, it is probably the Indonesian's strong obligation to gather following a death that puzzles the expatriate. The Indonesian is frustrated that the expatriate cannot immediately understand and honour the depth of feeling the situation commands.

There is not an expatriate in Indonesia who cannot tell of the servant or employee who appeared in a fluster, announced a death, said it was imperative he leave immediately, and hastened off— sometimes not to return for a week or more! Often and usually incorrectly, expatriates view these precipitous exits as transparent excuses for a holiday in the village. 'Very obliging father, dies regularly every summer,' is the sort of caustic comment one hears.

Please understand how important, how proper, how honour-giving it is to drop everything and go immediately to be with the family of the deceased. 'It is what we must do,' repeated our Indonesian sources.

A foreigner working in Central Java was killed in an accident. Funeral arrangements were handled by expatriates at the site and all his Indonesian co-workers attended the services. Later, Indonesians on the staff learnt that some friends of the deceased living in Jakarta had not been notified of the death. It was beyond their understanding that with easy telephone communication, efforts had not been made to notify everybody known to the deceased. This was considered a major breach of good manners.

Providing Perspective

It is helpful to contrast this with the high degree to which death formalities are handled outside the home by professionals in western countries. The funeral home, clergymen and florists take responsibility for the rituals, leaving the family to deal with their grief privately. Generally, it would be uncommon for anyone who is not an immediate family member to appear unannounced at the home of the deceased. Visiting and calling are formalised and observed by sending a gift of food or a card to the home, but not necessarily by making a personal call.

In Indonesia, exactly the opposite happens. While there are burial societies, their primary function is to serve as savings groups against the sudden expenses of death. Almost all the death formalities are handled by the immediate family with the emotional support of as many friends, relatives and associates as can crush into the house. Everyone is expected to appear!

Death—the Islamic Community

While there may be some regional differences in the *adat* (traditional behaviour), in general this is the agenda for most Muslim burials. From death to the grave is rarely more than 24 hours. To show great

Everyone hurries to the home of the deceased to participate in the prayers and to be with the family. Friends, neighbours and government officials came to mourn the death of former Vice-President Adam Malik.

honour to the deceased, an Indonesian responds to news of the death by appearing quickly at the home. Time available for the ceremonies is limited and the family can use help in the myriad activities that follow.

Meninggal! He is Dead

News of death is usually carried to close relatives and neighbours personally or by word of mouth. Telephones will jingle through the day or night to notify everyone possible. Neighbours, relatives and friends gather at the house. In a short time the ritual materials are gathered, and the body is washed and prepared for burial.

With all the immediate family in attendance, the body is taken outside, stripped and laid across banana tree trunks. A religious person (a Haji or an official from the mosque) massages the abdomen to empty the intestines and the body is bathed in water scented with flower petals or perfumed water. The religious person may ask the closest relative to pour the last water, to ensure that the memory of the deceased does not disturb the survivors.

The body is then placed on a *tikar* (woven mat), ceremonially wrapped in white cloth of specific lengths and packed with clean cotton, mothballs, crushed roses, eau-de-cologne—all to ensure that it is sweet smelling. Spiced cotton is placed under the armpits and the buttocks and on top of the body. The hands are crossed, right over left, and each of the three layers of cloth is tied about the body. When the wrapping is complete, those present will pray.

The body is lifted on to a *kurung batang* (a metal frame provided by the mosque) and transported to the cemetery on the shoulders of family members or in a vehicle. In the event of the death of a small child, it is common for the father to carry it in his arms to the grave site.

The equivalent of the western funeral is the *pemakaman*, the service at the grave site. As many people as possible go to the cemetery, the rental of vehicles being the gift of a family member or close friend. The vehicles often have large blue and white floral sprays attached to them. The male family members usually accompany the body, the women following in other vehicles. At the cemetery people stand in groups, the men separate from the women, although this custom is changing in some areas.

The body is placed in the grave with the head facing Mecca. The face cloth is lifted and the face 'kisses the soil'. Wooden planks are placed over the body like a tent and the relatives cast flower petals on this. Prayers are said and everyone adds a handful of soil to the grave. All are expected to stay until the grave is closed and shaped.

Mourning customs vary; many seem traditional and not directly related to Islamic practice. On Java, for instance, no photographs of the dead are displayed for at least 40 days. They are turned to the wall or left face down.

On the 3rd, 7th, 15th, 40th, 100th and 1000th days following the death there are prayers in the home led by a religious figure. Workers commonly take leave and return home to observe these prayers with as many family members as can gather there, especially for the 100th and 1000th day ceremonies. At this time the family may choose to send *besek-besek* (closed baskets containing a full meal with a dessert and fruit) to neighbours.

Etiquette in the Home

When you pay a condolence call (*melawat*) at the home, leave your shoes outside and wait to be seated, usually on the floor. Men sit cross-legged, women with legs to one side. It is possible that men and women will be seated separately.

Just inside the entrance will be a container partially filled with rice or something similar. Into this you place your gift of money (Rp. 5000–10,000) in a plain white envelope with your name inside. If the deceased is a neighbour rather than a business acquaintance or public servant, as soon as it is convenient, speak to their servants about sending food, or simply bring a kilo of tea or sugar for the family.

You will be served a small drink. Take it with a nod of acknowledgement. If you have arrived early you may stay for the prayers and accompany the group to the grave site. If the deceased has already been buried, after you have sipped your token drink and offered your condolences (see 'Words to Say'), ask permission to leave by saying '*Permisi* ...'.

Nothing but your presence is expected of you at the ceremonies. Logical or not, that alone has significance and meaning for the family. If you want to show great respect, visit the family late at night (10 p.m. or later), especially before the burial. There will be groups sitting with the body and praying. It is considered very good manners to say that you have come in the late evening because you wanted time with the family alone. Traditionally, the family should not sleep until the body is interred, so they are prepared to receive

157

guests at any time until all the rituals have been completed.

So great is the obligation for all friends and associates to be at the home of the deceased that it is quite common to see civil servants in government vehicles being transported on company time for the burial. This broad acknowledgement of the death of an ordinary person would be considered very exceptional in the west.

Reflecting on the hundreds of people who visited when her prominent economist father died, an Indonesian friend recalls her mother saying of an associate, 'Oh, forget him. He didn't even come to the house …'. Her mother has a memory like a trap for such events! So do most Indonesians.

Dressing Correctly

Men should wear a long-sleeved shirt and dark trousers. Women should dress conservatively in dark colours. Women do not wear jewellery or bright colours—red, pink, orange or yellow.

Do/Taboo

- Wait quietly if you are in doubt and someone will assist you. Watch carefully the way that people around you are behaving and do the same.
- Do not initiate action.
- Offer a gentle handshake or the traditional Asian greeting of palms pressed together and raised as you enter the house.
- Pay your call as a couple rather than have the woman go alone. (Exception: in the event of the death of a servant, it is acceptable for the expatriate woman as the obvious employer to pay a brief call immediately upon hearing of the death. It would also be appreciated if the husband and wife pay a call at the home together as soon as possible.)
- Say the formal words to express grief. (See 'Words to Say'.)
- Do not say '*Selamat*' and do not smile.

Vocabulary

Meninggal	To die. *Mati* is used commonly and imprecisely by many expatriates. Flowers and animals *mati*, humans *meninggal*.
Mobil Jenazah	Hearse.
Tanda berduka cita	The little yellow paper flags posted along the street to indicate the home of the deceased. They are also carried at the head of the procession taking the body to the graveyard.

Words to Say (or write)

All the words of condolence that follow are correct for the bereaved of any religion. The predictable Indonesian response is to nod and say '*Terima kasih.*' Do not expect protracted conversation.

Kami menghasurkan belasungkawa kami.
We join you in grieving.

Kami turut berduka cita.
We want to share in your sorrow.

Semoga arwahnya diterima di sisi Tuhan yang Maha Esa.
May his spirit be received by God.

In addition, the following Arabic words are often heard at the death of Muslims:
Inna lillahi wa inna ilaihi rojiun.
May he rest in peace next to God.

It is correct to write the following on a card: *Jika ada sesuatu yang dapat kami lalukan, kami harap jangan ragu-ragu untuk memberitahukannya.* (If there is anything we can do for you, please do not hesitate to let us know.)

Death—the Christian Community

In most cases, the deceased Christian will be kept in the family home in a coffin with desiccants and dry ice to preserve the body. Condolence calls would follow the same general form discussed previously. The minister of the church might lead the services in the home or, if the family wishes, in church.

Christian funeral services are a mix of customs left over from colonial times, *adat* of the ethnic group, church ritual, and current trends. An example of the latter is the recent (within the last ten years) appearance of photographers and persons making videotapes of the congregation during the service. This allows the family, at a later time, to know who came.

The expatriate could send flowers (tell the florist it is for a Christian funeral), money in a plain white envelope if the family can use it, or tea and sugar to supplement the refreshments for those who call. Your presence is appreciated most of all.

Suggestions for appropriate dress and words of condolence given previously are valid in this situation as well.

Death—the Chinese Community

This section describes the customs pertaining among non-Christian Chinese and provides guidelines for social calls on the family.

It would be considered bad manners to attend to the rituals of anyone, especially a prominent person, hastily. Several days may pass to allow the family members to gather before the body is cremated or buried. It is also possible that an auspicious day will be set for the funeral. In the interim, the body may be packed in dry ice with tea leaves used as a desiccant, and camphor balls, tuberose (*sedap malam*) and incense may be put around the room to keep the air fresh. A large photograph of the deceased is usually displayed at the foot of the coffin.

Most large Chinese communities have a crematorium. Ashes can be kept in a *rumah abu* (ash house), on the family altar in the home, or scattered in the sea. Clan associations of ethnic groups may give financial help to the families.

Some families observe the need for mourning clothes. Practices vary. Some wear garments of unbleached muslin inside out, others drape their heads with thick white jute or calico cloth. Most of the immediate family will wear a black patch pinned to the right sleeve of their garments and not wear red clothes for a set period of time.

While one may be notified personally of the death of a Chinese friend, the newspaper announcement, giving the venue of the wake and the date of the cremation or burial, is the family's signal that they are ready to receive visits of condolence from friends.

If the body of the deceased is in the home, you may expect to be met at the door by a family member who will assist you to observe the formalities and convey condolences to the family. You would probably be invited to have light refreshments before you leave.

If the body of the deceased is at the hospital, the setting is much more like a receiving line. You would probably be asked to drop by the home for refreshments following the cremation or burial.

Some families may engage professional mourners.

Do/Taboo

- Wear dark clothes, avoiding red and yellow. Women should wear no jewellery or make-up.
- Keep shoes on, unless you see that others are removing theirs.
- Do not help yourself to food until invited.
- At no time make death a personal issue; always refer to it in the third person: 'If a person were to die ...'
- Give money in a plain white envelope with your name on the outside only if the family needs financial assistance. In that case, Rp. 30,000–40,000 is appropriate. If the family is well to do, then a floral wreath, not a bouquet, is sent to the home with a card.
- The family or close friends of the deceased will not eat noodles, as it is thought to lengthen the period of sorrow.

161

Words to Say (on cards).
Turut berduka cita sedalam-dalam. (Deepest sympathy.)
Belasungkawa. (Sympathy.)

CARING FOR THE SPIRITS

The variety of grave-tending and spirit-caring activities that are observed throughout Indonesia literally describe cultures from the Stone Age to high-tech 20th century. The constant theme, regardless of the manner of expression, is one of reverential concern.

On Java, one will encounter the ceremony of *nyekar*, paying homage to the deceased at the grave site. It is considered traditional although the origins are not clear. Families will gather to clean the graves and put out flowers just before Lebaran.

In addition, for many ethnic groups it is considered mandatory to visit the graves of relatives at regular intervals or if passing through town.

Among the Indonesian Chinese there is a ceremony to mark the end of the mourning period. After that, it is the responsibility of the remaining family to perform at the grave site the ceremonies for the spirits of the dead. This varies from group to group.

The Balinese maintain temples for a variety of spirits. Most villages have a *pura dalem* or temple of the dead. Among some of the more primitive groups the bodies of the dead are kept in the living quarters and cared for until the ritual ceremonies can be performed to release the spirit.

If the expatriate encounters any of these activities, respectful behaviour is appreciated. Ask before you take photos and honour a refusal. Avoid climbing trees, walls and monuments for better camera angles if there are priests or religious officials present; their status demands that there should be none above them, literally.

Chapter Eight

TRANSLATING NEEDS INTO ACTION

It would seem that in one of the most densely populated countries in the world—Indonesia—there must be sheets, towels, soap powder, dishes and the myriad material comforts for body and soul. Generally, Jakarta and the half-dozen other large cities are considered very up-to-date, veritable glass and chrome repositories of the western brand-name goods that soothe the frazzled foreign nerves.

Generally, that is true. It is also true that most needs can be met practically wherever you live in Indonesia, with some concession to colour, size and brand. Genuine lacks are few; the opportunity for compromise is great.

163

Therefore, if you find yourself in a *becak* sloshing through the floods trying to find a house that does not dissolve in the rains, we hope that the information in this chapter will help you translate your needs into action. Some of the material is Jakarta-specific. Other information is of general value. Special data is inserted and clearly marked for 'the provinces'.

ACCOMMODATION

Indonesia has a growing number of international class hotels, a good range of clean, middle-class family hotels, recently constructed apartment and condominium complexes, and a wide selection of some of the most expensive home rentals in the world.

In the hotels of Jakarta and in the other international class hotels in the country, real estate agents prowl. They will usually find you long before you can even whimper the word, 'house'.

Folktales circulate about kitchens a day's hike from the main house and bedrooms whose doors all open to the outdoors. Happily, there are also available homes of a reasonable size whose floor plans reflect the general western living style and whose price, while as much as a mind-numbing US$2000 plus a month (in Jakarta), satisfies your company's criteria.

Housing in the Provinces

There are really two standards for housing: Jakarta and 'the rest'. Rents in the provinces are significantly lower. The houses are usually smaller than those found in the cities and they fall somewhere between Indonesian and western design. This means there will be an attached bath and kitchen. However, expatriates almost always install pedestal toilets. Towels almost always are hung and stored outside the bathroom.

Renovations in the kitchen include adding cupboards, stainless steel sinks and creating space for a refrigerator and a western stove. Indonesians store their kitchen equipment on racks and shop daily so they feel little need for storage space. It is important to remember that houses built for foreign aid experts are intended to be used later by Indonesian staff so they are built to Indonesian standard.

Hotels in the Provinces

Hotels here are often the venue chosen for entertaining, both by Indonesian counterparts and the foreign guest. (Remember that private homes are often small and the family may consist of many generations.)

Housing Districts

In Jakarta, high expatriate populations are in Menteng near the business district, and the 'suburbs' of Kebayoran Baru, Kemang, Kemang Indah, Simpruk, Pertamina Oil Village, Kuningan and Permata Hijau. All these places house a mixture of upper- and middle-class Indonesians and foreigners.

The sections in the south—Cilandak, Cipete, Pondok Indah, Country Woods Estate, Bintaro, and Lebak Bulus—are nearer the Jakarta International School and the Japanese School and have access to the new ring roads that provide access to the new system of toll roads. Most of these areas now enjoy other suburban amenities—western-style shopping centres, branches of banks, hospitals, and postal facilities.

Inspecting Potential Housing

Wherever you find yourself, if the accommodation has not been provided by your employer, check the following as you inspect your potential home:

1 Creatures that eat your house

Dainty piles of fine sawdust and timber that you can push your thumbnail through are clues to the presence of *rayap* (termites). Consider a regular spraying service or renting another house.

165

2 Domestic water

In the cities some homes have partial municipal water service and some have wells with electric or hand pumps. Most homes are equipped with water storage facilities.

Environmental and industrial pollution has devastated the purity of water in almost all of Indonesia. Urban pollution is reflected in the fact that the majority use the river water indiscriminately to bathe, wash, dispose of garbage and relieve themselves. Bottled water is readily available, packaged by the glass, the litre, or delivered to your home or office complete with dispenser that provides the liquid either boiled or chilled.

In Jakarta, a sample of your tap water (which may be part of the municipal water supply or from a private well) can be taken to the Perusahan Air Minum office to be analysed.

3 Electricity

The introduction of electricity into the cities of Indonesia—most of it accomplished since 1945—has been uneven. It is possible to have both 220 and 110 volt circuits in your home! Efforts are being made country-wide to standardise the power supply to 220 volts, 50 cycle, to stabilise power supply and to upgrade service.

Inquire from neighbours about the area's history of power cuts and 'brown-outs'. Although power cuts are increasingly infrequent, you may want to keep kerosene lamps, candles, or flashlights for emergencies. Consider buying voltage regulators to protect the major appliances from damage in 'power sags'.

Cooking is usually done with bottled gas although electric microwave units are seen now in the larger cities.

Beware of shocking accidents: Residents in Indonesia tend to forget that the combination of bare feet and wet surfaces can be lethal when one is flipping electrical switches or working with electric machines, few of which are earthed.

Indonesian householders routinely undertake much of their own minor electrical repairs. Cord is available by the mile and the variety of plugs, sockets, switches, and electrical bits and pieces is mind-boggling. Chances are you, too, will be wiring up lamps and attempting minor household electrical repairs.

Unfortunately, domestic and office staff have a serendipitous tendency to perform these repairs with cellophane, adhesive or masking tape and elastic bands. They frequently pull the plug from the socket by the cord with electrifying results! On occasion, one sees the 'wash girl' happily ironing, with the bare cord emitting a spray of sparks. It is the householder's responsibility to check appliances and their wiring.

Dealing with the electric company: The state-owned electric company, PLN (Perusahaan Listrik Negara), is actively trying to upgrade its service. When requesting assistance in person or on the phone, be prepared to give your name and address, telephone number, and a statement of the problem in Bahasa Indonesia.

In the larger cities, PLN will normally respond to a call within several hours. In the provinces it may be necessary to appear in person at the office to emphasise the request for service. If the electrical outage is in a general area, you will be informed. If the problem is only at your residence, when the work is done, you will be asked to sign the report. A small tip or *wang rokok* (cigarette money) to the PLN repairman is appreciated, but not mandatory.

Before you move in, determine where and when the bill should be paid.

Electricity in the provinces: Electricity is usually very low capacity, but sometimes this can be increased. Realistic rather than wishful thinking about your electrical life will save you some frustrations. What do you need? What do you want? What is actually possible? Collect the facts and structure your needs on that.

4 Location
An inquiry about the flow of traffic and the times of traffic snarls

will give you a more realistic picture of how far you really are from the job or the schools. Most westerners try not to live too close to mosques. Prayers, amplified, begin at 4:30 every morning.

5 Neighbourhood responsibilities

As a new resident in the neighbourhood, it is your responsibility to *lapor* (check in with) the RT (Rukun Tetangga)—pronounced 'air tay'—the elected chairman of your neighbourhood association. This should be done before one month passes. While the efficiency and energy of the RTs may vary, they are responsible for the activities and concerns of the neighbourhood.

6 Plumbing and waste disposal

Flush the toilets and check the pressure of all the water taps in your prospective home. Because municipal waste treatment facilities are not common in Indonesia, most home owners rely on septic tanks which must be routinely pumped out by the JINJA trucks (septic tank service of the municipalities). The effluvia is almost always discharged, untreated, into the rivers.

7 Repairs

It is an acceptable practice to withhold some of the advance rent (which is often as much as three years!) against the completion of the remodelling and repairs promised by the landlord.

8 Security

Barred doors and windows are optional. One should check carefully for access to the roof, the condition of fences and gates, and the effectiveness of yard lights. Most householders hire night guards (*jaga malam*) and usually the RT of the neighbourhood will employ roving night watchmen (*Hansip*) who work from a central point (*Pos Siskamling*). The money collected monthly from the entire neighbourhood pays their salaries.

9 Servants' quarters

They should have their own entrance, private rooms and separate bathing and cooking areas.

10 Telephones

Most people look for a house with a phone already installed. This simplifies the situation greatly. The government has made increased communication capabilities a priority and the use of the Palapa satellite has improved the situation in many areas. International Direct Dialling facilities and public pay phones are now available in many cities.

Generally, phones are listed under the name of the house owner. This causes two obvious problems: first, if you are renting a home the number will probably not be listed in your (the user's) name; second, it is possible you will get a fair number of calls for the house owner whom you may or may not know.

Seasonal heavy rains, lightning strikes, the occasional rodent or falling tree all seem to have laid devious plots against the health of the phone lines. Lines get crossed and it is possible to have several conversations at once in several languages. The repair services are rapidly improving.

Telephones in the provinces: The usual rule is, if you rent a house with one in it then you have one. To get one installed is usually difficult, expensive and involves a long wait. Some options might be to use the phone at the hotel or see if your company has made arrangements for alternative phone service. Have reasonable expectations.

11 Screens

They are the easiest way to protect against mosquitoes. In theory, most of the large cities are malaria-free. (The malaria-carrying mosquitoes prefer to breed in rice paddies and brackish waters.) In Bali, the malarial mosquito is coastal breeding and the transmission of malaria is common there. Be warned: mosquitoes carry a wide variety of dread diseases other than malaria, one of which is dengue haemorrhagic fever.

12 Walls and ceilings
Look for the grey-black smudge of mildew that suggest your roof or walls leak.

13 Who's responsible?
Some houses come furnished or partly furnished. Be sure you understand clearly what the rent covers. Who pays the maintenance and/or repairs on the house? Homes in Indonesia, if unfurnished, can mean exactly that! Sometimes, even the light fixtures need to be supplied by the tenant.

CLIMATE
Tropic is guaranteed; paradise is not! The climate in Indonesia provides a predictable routine of:
- High humidity. About 75 per cent day and night.
- Heat. Countrywide, the temperature is 30-34°C (86–93°F). In the mountains you may experience a chilling 18–22°C (64–72°F) and finally get to wear your sweater!
- Two seasons. Wet (*musin hujan*), September to February; and dry (*musin kemarau*) from March to August. Or wetter and wet.
- Days of equal length and little variety. The sun rises about 6 a.m. and sets in sunsets of magenta and pink from the dust of volcanoes, obligingly at about 6 p.m. daily.

Three Important Health Guards
The most important concerns are:
1. Regular, moderate exercise: You may want to get out early in the cool of the day to jog, walk the dog, cycle or join the Hash House Harriers, a made-in-Asia group of recreational runners.

In the larger cities, health clubs are appearing and you can exercise in the comfort of airconditioning. Any way you take it, do exercise regularly.

2. Adequate fluid intake: Residents and travellers are advised to drink plenty of fluids—water is best.

3. Reasonable lifestyle: Consider bringing your day forward by rising and going to bed earlier. As an alternative, consider adopting the habit of napping in the afternoon.

Two-temperature Worlds

With the common use of airconditioning, a temperate climate work situation is created in many offices and homes. For most expatriates, this familiar setting ameliorates the enervating effects of heat.

The assumption in our modern environment is that everyone has access to airconditioning. And this, of course, is not true. Most of the Indonesian work force is affected by two climates, the non-airconditioned reality of their personal lives and the temperature and humidity controlled setting of their work lives. *Nyonya* may wish to reflect on this as she emerges from her airconditioned nest in the heat of the afternoon and finds the workmen sleeping in the cool of the garage!

Climate probably affects some traditional values. Because the harsh winter of the northern hemisphere never comes here, there is no sense of urgency about getting something done before a season changes. Hence, 'Tomorrow is O.K.'

CLOTHING

Fortunately, neither the demands of modernity nor the traditional culture calls for anything other than reasonable, modest apparel. The influence of Islam is felt in the standards and styles for women. Shoulders are to be covered and extreme styles (shorts, stretch strapless tank tops, wild disco styles) are generally frowned on in public. Many women feel they are being attacked by a vengeful,

171

sticky slip on a hot day, and it is well to line dresses with light cotton voile so that they are not transparent.

Many Indonesians told us that, in general, they form their opinion about the total lifestyle of the expatriate by observing his clothing. 'Do all people look like that in your country?' was asked again and again. This bears repeating here: the expatriate, willingly or unwillingly, is seen as a representative of his country.

The style of dress is casual and comfortable and really 'dress-up' events are rare. The most formal attire for a man is a business suit and for women an afternoon tea dress or a short evening dress.

Most foreigners and Indonesians have their clothes made here. The tailors and sewing ladies are skilful and charge reasonable prices. And with servants to attend to the ironing, maintaining cotton garments is no longer a personal pact with heavy labour.

There is a growing ready-made clothing industry. Most of a person's total wardrobe needs are available here with some limits on colour and style in the larger sizes. Indonesia is famed for the beauty of its traditional cloth, *batiks* and silks. It is also one of the Southeast Asian centres for the production of textiles for the world market.

Vocabulary

Below is a rough guide to the dress code on official invitations:

Batik	Men should appear in a long-sleeved *batik* shirt and women in a good dress, in a dark colour, with sleeves.
Lounge suit	The most formal wear for men (western business suit and tie) if the setting is *acara rasmi* (very formal). A woman should wear a good dress, as described above.
PSH	*Pakaian Sipil Harian* describes the 'regular' civil servant 'uniform', a short-sleeved safari suit.
PSL	*Pakaian Sipil Lengkap* means 'complete'. A western man would be correct in a dark business suit, white shirt and tie. Indonesian officials entitled to wear military or police uniform would do so.

PSR   *Pakaian Sipil Rasmi.* The Indonesian civil servant would appear in a long-sleeved safari suit. It also means 'uniform'. A foreigner entitled to wear an official (military) uniform would be correct to do so.

You will notice, on the 17th of each month, that government employees usually gather outside the buildings early in the morning before the workday begins for a short ceremony (reflecting on the Independence Day of August 17th). Each civil servant wears a shirt or blouse of the same *batik* print. The effect is impressive.

HOSPITALS

Medical care is a concern for everyone. Most people want to be assured of the quality of care that they will receive in an emergency. For the expatriate, this begins with a brief understanding of how the system works here and how he needs to be prepared.

All hospitals are supposed to give emergency care without presentation of documents or proof of ability to pay.

Prepare Your Documents

Present at least a copy of your passport, KIM (immigration card), and a fair amount of cash. One routinely pays a cash deposit on admission. Be prepared to speak Bahasa Indonesia or take someone who can assist you. Hysterical babbling in any language will not serve you well.

Prepare Your Expectations

Some of the aspects of hospitalisation that the westerner finds most reassuring don't exist here in quite the same form. In general:

1. Don't expect the hospital to file insurance claims. They usually, however, assist you to compile information.
2. Do realise that in some hospitals the family may be expected to buy medicine and equipment necessary for the patient's care and bring it to the hospital.

173

3. Not all hospitals routinely provide meals. It is much more common to have the food brought from home.
4. The atmosphere of enforced hushed quiet is noticeably lacking in most Indonesian hospitals. It is expected that the entire family and all friends will rally around the bed of the sick.
5. The most common form of accommodation is a bed in a ward.

There are exceptions to all the above observations, particularly in private missionary hospitals and some private hospitals in the larger cities, but do not expect the exception.

Note: If your servants fall ill and need to be hospitalised, remember that many of them have a dread fear that they are being sent there to die. This fear is related to the fact that in the countryside, traditional medicine is usually attempted first and, in many cases, by the time the patient is brought to the hospital, death is unavoidable.

Hospitals in Jakarta

The following are hospitals frequently used by foreigners. Choose a familiar hospital. In a life-threatening situation, go to the nearest.

Town Centre
- St. Carolus
  Jl. Salemba Raya 41, Menteng, Tel: 8580091 (Emergency room)
- Dr. Cipto Mangunkusumo ICCU (recommended for cardiac cases)
  Jl. Diponegoro 69, Menteng, Tel: 334636

West Jakarta
- Sumber Waras
  Jl. Kyai Tapa, Grogol, Tel: 596011

South Jakarta
- Pertamina
  Jl. Kyai Maja 43, Kebayoran Baru, Tel: 707211 (Emergency room)

- Rumah Sakit Pondok Indah
  Jl. Metro Dua, Kav UE, Tel: 7697525
- Rumah Sakit Setia Mitra
  Jl. R.S. Fatmawati 80-82, Cilandak, Tel: 7696000

Hospitals in the Provinces

In the provinces, where police are called to (traffic) accidents, the victims must go to an RSU (Rumah Sakit Umum, the public hospital). These usually have the least equipment to handle accident trauma victims. The doctor is not always available and the medic on duty may be only trained in first aid. The care is often well intended but poorly skilled. Here, more than anywhere else, it seems that having a personal contact or personal influence will get assistance.

Medical Care Outside Jakarta

This list of hospitals is not complete and is meant only as a guide. If you find yourself in the provinces without someone you know to assist you, ask for help from the police or an official:

1. In a provincial capital, go to the Department of Health, Kantor Dinas Kesehatan Propinsi.
2. In a regency capital, ask for the Kantor Dinas Kesehatan Kabupaten.
3. In the smaller towns, ask for the Puskesmas or government health centre. Don't expect any of them to observe western working hours.

Bandung, West Java
- The Adventist Hospital
  (mission hospital, English-speaking staff) Jl. Cihampelas

Bali
- Bali General Hospital
  Sanglah, Denpasar

175

Bogor, West Java
* The Red Cross Hospital
  Jl. Raya Pajajaran (near the Botanical Gardens)

Bukit Tinggi, Central Sumatra
* Immanuel Hospital
  (mission hospital, English-speaking staff) Jl. Sudirman

LIBRARIES

Throughout the islands, most schools for expatriates have libraries which are accessible to the parents of enrolled children. Various government agencies and some private companies maintain libraries that can be tapped by the public. In the provinces, libraries are part of the facilities of large companies that provide on-site accommodation for employers. Special interest clubs and social and cultural organisations are usually a source of reading material.

Libraries in Jakarta

The following libraries are open to the public:
* Australian Cultural Centre
  Citibank Building, 5th Floor, Jl. M.H. Thamrin 55, Menteng, Tel: 330824. This has an English language library of 5000 titles and 250 magazines and periodicals.
* The British Council
  Widjojo Centre, Jl. Jenderal Sudirman 56 (Senayan), Tel: 587411
  This has an English language library of about 20,000 titles. There is also a British Council Library in Bandung, West Java.
* Erasmus Huis
  Jl.Rasuna Said (Kuningan), Tel: 512321
  This has a Dutch language library of approximately 10,000 titles.
* French Cultural Centre
  Jl. Salemba Raya 25 (Salemba), Tel: 881623
  This has a library of French language titles.

- Goethe Institute
  Jl. Mataram Raya 23 (Jatinegara), Tel: 882798. This has a German language library of approximately 10,000 books, 50 periodicals and several newspapers.
- Indonesian American Cultural Centre
  Jl. Pramuka, Kav 20 (Jatinegara), Tel: 881241. This has an English language library of approximately 10,000 titles and a quantity of reference materials on Indonesia.
- Japan Cultural Centre
  Jl. Cemara 1 (Menteng), Tel: 324658. This has a number of activities and services available to the public, including the library and the audio-visual room.

THE MYTH OF BOUNTY

Indonesia's tropical setting does not imply limitless fertility of the land. Contrary to popular opinion, the soil on the islands as a whole is not particularly fertile. Bali and Java create that illusion. Bali has three growing seasons—it is said that you can hear the crops grow there! Java is really the market garden of Indonesia.

Three major factors limit the fertility of the land and influence the availability of food countrywide. First is the impact of events of nature—floods, volcanoes, insects, drought. Second, traditionally foods are ripe when harvested and sold or consumed in the area in which they are grown. (Jakarta is the exception to this, often advertising the availability of fruits from other areas. (See 'Food, Wonderful Food!'.) The third factor is that throughout Indonesia farm to market roads have not yet been well developed.

In comparison with the 'outer islands', Java has a good system of roads and rails. Bali has an improving system of roads and the Trans-Sumatra highway was opened recently. However, the combination of almost biodegradable roads and bridges and the inability of the small farmer to pay shipping costs makes it more to his advantage to sell the produce locally.

In a typical street market, vendors spread their wares as space allows. Hence, bananas, rice, chillies, chairs, dish racks, and probably cooked snacks share the space to attract buyers.

Thus Indonesians and expatriates at factory sites, oil camps, and in small towns in the provinces complain about the occasional poor quality, high cost, and interrupted availability of fruit and vegetables in the markets. Foods common in one area cannot always be grown easily in another, and in many areas it is possible to have a good choice only of seasonal items.

Shopping in the Provinces

The supermarket chain has arrived on the 'inner islands' and seems to be expanding throughout the provinces, bringing with it some fast food chains. Small groceries, some equipped with airconditioning, refrigerators and freezers, make available a good if erratic selection of processed foods and personal care products. The availability of imported goods is a bit more sporadic.

Dairy products are difficult to find and expensive. Tins of processed cheese and butter are generally available. Local ham, bacon and sausages are rare. Expatriates commonly buy goats and chickens to slaughter for their personal use.

STORING YOUR EMOTIONAL BAGGAGE ... (especially in the provinces!)

Your physical life in the provinces will be as pleasant as you are able to make it. It is a fact of expatriate life that most of them spend a lot of time and energy trying to make their home here as similar as possible to their home there.

Keeping Your Emotional Balance

Your emotional life is prey to distress that is sometimes severe, sometimes a nagging irritation and sometimes humorous. We have found that most of these moments are exacerbated by two feelings: guilt and distance from 'home'.

Guilt: Parents with school-age children who find themselves in the 'home-teaching' position, with unrealistic expectations about the mother's ability to be both teacher and mother, or find only the presence of brave, often makeshift camp or company schools, sometimes feel great guilt that they are depriving their children of a 'normal' childhood—peers, computers, TV trends, friends and relations, awareness of current events, youth clubs, suburban neighbourhoods, sports teams, etc. This feeling seems to be most common with expatriates who are on short-term assignments of one to two years.

One missionary child related her memory of her mother kneeling in prayer, a small child on each side, asking, 'Please God, give me the patience to teach my children.'

Some parents feel guilt that (selfishly) they have chosen to indulge their sense of adventure to travel, or need to follow a job, with the children following as unwilling baggage.

People are unnerved by the awareness that new cultures to encounter, new countries to see, new languages to learn are just that: these rarely compensate for anything else missed. The sense of being deprived of what is 'due you' in your own culture remains and is not lessened by tons of wild orchids or years of magenta sunsets.

Distance: The great distance from home becomes a major factor for emotional pain when letters arrive with 'guilt-tickets' in them … too bad you missed your class reunion, the grandchild's baptism, a beautiful spring, the 20th century! Whatever, it's hard to handle.

It helps to remember that even at home, most of us live a fair distance from the rest of our families. We would probably miss some of these events no matter where we were living. What seems to bring distress may be the combination of physical distance and the fact that you, the expatriate, chose to leave them and embrace the gracious expatriate life.

You are reminded, not to subtly …

- that it is too bad you are missing a major family event—a wedding, a birth—but everyone knows if you could, you would really want to be there (which may or may not be true).
- of the sense of wistful bravery in the face of a family crisis and the implication (which may or may not be true) that it would have been lessened or averted by your presence—the lingering death of a venerably aged family member, the wild behaviour swings of a teenager.
- that something that is an emotional anchor for you has been dislodged—your beloved cat died, your home was burgled, someone demolished your car, your favourite roses died in a hard winter because you weren't there to mulch them in.

There is also the ethnocentric tendency to feel that a dreadful situation here would not exist there. For example, if the treasured infant of one of your Indonesian staff/friends/colleagues dies needlessly from an illness bred by poor sanitation, the comment of a local health officer, 'Many people in the area are still not used to boiling their water and washing their hands before eating,' may provoke in you angry comparisons and broadly focused rage fed by the intense and irrational feeling, 'This would never happen at home.' In a stressful setting, people tend to over-reaction in situations that normally would produce none. For example, squabbles between a couple of 5-year-olds are taken up by the parents. This outrageous and childish behaviour takes the place of the gentle and supportive neighbourliness that is really needed.

National holidays (yours), especially if there is a great family tradition associated with them, can tear you apart. It does not serve you well to remark with wistful frequency on Grandmother's wonderful roast turkey if you are challenged to do something miraculous with an athletic chicken lying in muscular *rigor mortis* on your kitchen table.

Some families report great success in improvising to create new traditions. Others suggest that first, you affirm to yourselves the validity of your choice to live for a period of time away from 'home' and then celebrate, but not too close to the 'traditional' ways. The heroic attitude is difficult to maintain. When the adrenalin wears off and routine sets in, it becomes a burden.

Assumptions about Expatriates

People the world over are often surprised to realise the difference between how they see themselves and their motives for behaviour and how others perceive those same aspects. Unfortunately, none of us reads minds, and so we must establish our relationships on what we assume and perceive to be truthful observations about others.

We end this section with comments that reflect how the expatriate is viewed generally in the provinces.

He is presumed to be:

- a person of status;
- smarter (an expert!) and richer than the local population; and
- coming from a more developed culture.

Indonesian ideas of most westerners are shaped by the appearance and behaviour of tourists, grade B movies and improbable television series. So expatriates are seen as:

- possessed with unlimited resources;
- incredibly clever—never without an answer or solution!
- uniformly beautiful; and
- free (of many of the local *adat* or traditional laws of behaviour), especially sexually free.

This 'assumed' western behaviour and appearance is perceived as a challenge by many Indonesians. Some try to tap the bounty that you seemingly possess. Others may be intimidated by all the assumed western attributes and respond by meekness and close to zero productivity for fear of doing anything that would incur your wrath.

In the provinces, too, the expatriate is not expected to understand the native or the social system. He is thus excused for making social blunders. All this allows you to escape the pressure of adapting and coping, but it can also prevent you from really entering and enjoying the rich local culture.

TRANSPORTATION

We list some of the common forms of transportation you might find yourself on, in the cities and in the countryside. Most inter-city buses have set fares (subject to change) and most of smaller, privately owned conveyances charge negotiable fares on a trip by trip basis. One buys one-way and not round-trip train tickets. Touts buy blocks of tickets for resale at higher prices, especially during the holidays.

If you are attempting extensive travel using local facilities, prepare yourself by talking with someone who has done it, give yourself extra time for probable delays, and carry enough money to bail out and get home fast!

The Becak

The Indonesian trishaw or bicycle rickshaw known as the *becak* is

182

being legislated out of the larger cities because of the confusion it causes in the flow of traffic. However, it is alive and well in the smaller towns and villages. The *becak* is usually an inexpensive, comfortable, slow, congenial method of transportation. If your trip around town is short and time is plentiful, take a *becak*.

The Bemo

This small truck is similar to the jeepney of the Philippines. It runs regular routes almost round the clock. Just flag one down and pay your share of the route.

The *bemo* has benches down its length and passengers sit knee to knee. The conditions are crowded. It is possible to share the ride with chickens, pickpockets, sick children, and an occasional goat. One foreigner found himself in close quarters with a young man who was making personal advances. The westerner could only move his arm enough to get a grip on the other fellow's ear and smilingly suggest, '*Jangan!*' (Don't do that!) as he twisted the ear. The implication of course was that if he did not want to take his ear home in a box, he should keep his hands to himself.

The Colt

Minibuses, known familiarly as Colts, bump and lurch their way the absolute length of Indonesia, carrying cabbages, carrots, goats, people, coconuts—whatever is in transit. They are usually incredibly crowded, hot, slow and uncomfortable.

Travelling in one provides a great opportunity to practise your Bahasa Indonesia and experience life at the village level. It isn't fun; it just beat walking.

The Inter-City Bus

These overloaded carbon-spewing goliaths lurch from city to city carrying people and goods fairly quickly and at reasonable prices. There are usually some stops for food and a quick run to the WC.

183

Some of these vehicles are well maintained and reasonably comfortable. Many offer 'Full AC and Video!' Others are true 'chicken express' rolling piles of scrap that challenge the heart and good sense.

The Taxi

Generally speaking, the taxis are safe. They have a rather made-in-Asia attitude toward which side of the road they will stay on, and the speed limit. In the cities pay the fare on the meter. Tipping is up to you. Most taxi drivers expect a small tip.

In some areas taxis can be ordered by phone. They generally cruise the streets to pick up fares. In smaller towns, there are private cars which 'moonlight' as taxis. Contracting for their services usually means negotiations in Bahasa Indonesia.

It is your responsibility to have the money for the fare. Do not expect the taxi driver to be able to make change.

Do not assume that the taxi driver will know the address if it is in the least bit obscure. It will always help if you have the address written down. Most are willing to stop and ask for directions. They will usually do their best to get you where you want to go.

The Taxi Motorcycle—Ojek

A growing phenomenon are the motorcycle taxis, known as *ojek*. These cluster at road junctions. Passengers leaving buses at the main road negotiate for rides into the villages. It is helpful to know the language and have a fair idea of price before you begin to negotiate.

— Chapter Nine —

BUSINESS, INDONESIAN-STYLE

This is not a chapter on how to establish a business in Indonesia. There are mountains of manuals, a labyrinth of legalities, and legions of lawyers who must be consulted before embarking on a business venture here. The purpose of this chapter is to put into perspective some of the areas of social sensitivity about which the businessman will want to educate himself.

We begin with brief notes from history against which are placed statements from Indonesians about what their expectations are from expatriate 'experts'. Indonesian businessmen then list seven areas where the foreign businessman/technician often misreads the signals.

1. function of the *Bapak*-boss;
2. filter-factor or go-betweens;
3. need for oblique 'straight-talk';
4. elastic view of time;
5. need for consensus in decision-making;
6. protective labour laws and cultural view of dismissal; and
7. importance of the acknowledgement of nationalism.

For comparison, we have included a summary of the results of Dr Geert Hofstede's research regarding the pitfalls that exist for the Dutch (and most westerners) doing business in Indonesia.

Finally, there are some personal considerations, the answers to which affect both the expatriate's personal and business adjustment and efficiency here.

NOTES FROM PAST AND PRESENT

Professor Selo Soemardjan, a leading Indonesian sociologist, commented on business and culture in Indonesia in a recent presentation in Perth, Australia.

He reflected that in the past the colonial businessmen did not involve Indonesians in the management of their firms, or allow them policy-making positions. Nor did they entertain the thought that the economic systems of East and West would ever be compatible. Consequences of this attitude were a lack of awareness that the colonials' way of exploiting the natural and human resources was not congruent with the values of the local culture, and a lack of effort expended on either side for mutual understanding.

Bringing the situation into the present, another prominent Indonesian businessman remarked pointedly, 'The majority of the nationals feel that they have always been cheated by everyone who has done business in Indonesia. The nationals resent the "extraction" mentality, the "get-the-money-and-run" attitude, the short memory for friends and business contacts, and the ability to do business and not make it personal. We have learnt to be cautious.'

A successful Indonesian businessman added, 'In the west, strangers do business with strangers and the emphasis is on the excellence or suitability of the product. Here, we do business with friends. We may look like we are listening to the salesman's proposal and the list of qualities of his product. Actually, that isn't enough; the stage has not been set for business.'

INDONESIAN EXPECTATIONS

What does the Indonesian expect the expatriate to know about the personal style of doing business?

1. Business relationships are not democratic, they are hierarchical. In every situation you can immediately recognise who is the authority, who the subordinate. (A government official or civil servant, on almost any level, has the higher status.)
2. In the eyes of the Indonesian, the foreigner is primarily and always a guest.
3. Maintenance of face to face harmony of feelings will always take precedence over the task to be performed.

How do you achieve the Indonesian style of doing business?

1. By doing your homework. Assemble all the information that you can, be aware of government policy; check your data and determine from personal contacts what the other person's assumptions and expectations are.
2. Through experience and socialising. An Indonesian businessman related a tale of an expatriate who 'did not fit' and failed quickly in his attempt to work and live in Indonesia. He mentioned the following specific behaviour—blocks to the normal socialising that would have provided social support and experience:
   • A tendency to issue commands rather than develop supportive relationships.
   • An irrational fear of the food, water and living conditions that confused, insulted and finally alienated the nationals working

187

with him. 'We all want our food and living conditions to be clean and comfortable. He would demand that the egg be washed before it was boiled!'

- A need to be superior in knowledge and technical skill. This served to separate him from all his colleagues.

The replacement quickly learnt the language, socialised with the nationals and became part of both the project and the community of workers.

THE BOSS, THE BAPAK

The most significant figure in the hierarchy is the *bapak*. The attitude of *asal bapak senang* (keeping the boss—father—happy) is a *sine qua non* in Indonesian polite and business society. In any setting, the person who at that moment has the *bapak* role may expect deference and obedience.

Because of the 'father-child' relationship, discipline, for example, can be administered in a palatable form by the boss. Professor Soemardjan amplifies his comments on the interaction of culture with business: 'Being talked to (by the boss) in a private environment and in a quiet way makes him (the employee) feel like being talked to by his father. No Indonesian can harbour hard feelings against his father. This is a culturally determined relationship between father and son, which can also apply between a superior and subordinate in a company, an office, or a factory.'

This behaviour is relative and goes to the highest reaches of power. One prominent Indonesian businessman reminded that for every employee the boss is only a phone call away! 'The links in the chain are very, very close.' If the boss calls, he is obeyed. Other plans or appointments on the agenda will be put back. Everyone is always deferring to someone else.

The Indonesian Government Official

The Indonesian civil official is not considered a public civil servant.

He is the *tua* (headman, respected elder) and is accorded deep respect. It would be an error of judgement to give him orders or expect that he is there to serve you.

THE FILTER FACTOR

In all situations, especially in the higher circles, there is a need to be aware of the correct channels or access from you and your position to the person you wish to deal with.

The concept of having contacts, using a mentor, an adviser, a facilitator, a guide, an intermediary to filter thoughts and signals is centuries old and universally practised. In Indonesia it is a highly developed and essential aspect of doing business. The foreigner who lacks the appropriate personal relationship should inquire tactfully to find the 'right' intermediary. Highly placed officials are often used as facilitators to arrange introductions and interpret the prevailing business signals.

All Indonesians take another—the facilitator—with them when they pay official business calls. Our Indonesian friends tell us that since most of the decisions have already been made in careful, previous informal negotiations, the presence of a trusted intermediary makes the official meeting more relaxed.

The Secretary

'Never underestimate the power of a good secretary,' one businessman said seriously. 'She can make or break her boss by the way she deals with people.' A secretary is normally very protective and will screen calls or callers.

Sometimes a secretary survives several bosses in a position. She becomes a repository of information, names of contacts and general business wisdom. Her relationship with her boss is professional and confidential. Sometimes the boss will have his secretary ask another for information—about a situation, mood, feeling—relative to a business deal. This is standard business procedure in Indonesia.

189

GIVE IT TO ME STRAIGHT!

Bad news never travels upwards! However, if all reports are glowing and all news is good and everyone is happy, just how is bad news communicated?

The transmission of bad or contrary news has two requisites: first it is always done is private; second, it is always given by a trusted, confidential adviser. It is not uncommon for this person to be a relative as well as a business partner.

Professor Selo Soemardjan addresses this issue pointedly. 'Recognising the subtle feelings of the Indonesian, and particularly those of the Javanese, it is advisable never to make him ashamed in the presence of others.' It is a typical human response that shaming or embarrassing a person undermines his respectability or authority with those who witnessed the shaming.

TIME

Time is not a marketable commodity here. One neither buys it, saves it, wastes it, nor is a slave to it. Neither does time ever take precedence over the quality of the relationship. It has been said that a friend never needs an appointment. Neither is one hasty with a friend. The businessman who grumbles, 'I'm here to do business, not make friends,' will find that he has accomplished nothing.

Deadlines, Postponements and ...

Attitudes toward deadlines are extremely laid back. Because there is always the possibility that a project will be postponed, interrupted, neglected, rescheduled, forgotten, or cancelled, Indonesians hesitate to make a commitment.

There is a long tradition in Indonesia of being tolerant of delay. When this couples with the social value of deferring to authority, the western businessman, driven by punctuality, is left eating his hat in the lounge. Experience alone will help you assess what is 'important' and what can be forgotten readily.

THE NEED FOR CONSENSUS

From the fruit market to the board room, one bargains in Indonesia. In making agreements and deciding policy, the need to work out a collective agreement (*musyawarah untuk muafakat*) is almost as important as the quality of the personal relationship. This need for harmonious agreement will be part of business and also of interpersonal relationships between the domestic staff and the householder, and between friends.

It is important to note that consensus is practised when a number of departments or offices are involved in an issue; within the office, the authority of the *bapak* or father figure prevails.

The 'someone is going to win and it will be me' attitude is greatly at odds with the Indonesian way which does not see negotiations as a contest. The idea is to very carefully consider all issues and feelings so that everyone remains in a state of harmony and suffers no loss of face.

The Indonesians think it incongruous to stand and shake hands at the end of a bitter legal battle. 'No one wants to smile and shake hands if you feel that you have just lost,' commented an Indonesian lawyer, veteran of many bargaining sessions.

Successful Negotiation

An important part of negotiations is the lobbying beforehand. This is also done in the west; in Indonesia it is almost an art form. The formal business session may resemble a *sandiwara*—a play in which everyone speaks his polished part. If successfully done, there are no surprises, no anger, no sense of loss or exploitation. Usually everything has been settled before. The formal meeting is an elegant affirmation of the harmonious agreement of the members.

Hidden Agenda

If all the business is not settled in a meeting, the foreigner might begin to encounter excuses offered by his Indonesian counterparts.

191

Then, instead of becoming more aggressive, the expatriate should back off and consider renewed informal negotiations.

Staying in the Channels

Often the process for translating decisions into action is one that is obliged to stay in proper channels, to observe proper forms in proper order, and to work through a series of officials. Lower level officials slow the flow of paper because of their reluctance to take responsibility and their tendency to cling to procedure even when dispensation has been issued to expedite a situation.

A long-time foreign resident's experience with a lost passport illustrates this. When the loss was reported to the Immigration officials, the supervisor kindly offered a special letter to expedite the paperwork. When the expatriate showed the letter, all the clerks and minor officials agreed that it was valid and would be helpful, but it was not procedure! Expatriate and Indonesian alike speculate that this conservative and hesitant attitude can be traced to job protection.

PROTECTIVE LABOUR LAWS

After the Second World War, Indonesia, eager to participate positively in world affairs, joined the International Labour Organisation. The result was new legislation in women and child labour laws which followed international standards.

Control over adherence to labour legislation does not cover all companies. The main targets are the bigger (and almost always multinational) companies. Restrictions regarding termination of employment were passed in the 1950s. To dismiss an employee, the permission of the local labour office must be secured. The law also requires that each company affected by the labour laws produce a personnel manual that meets the approval of the labour office.

Because the laws are conservative, companies have adopted several informal methods of 'encouraging termination'. One of the most common is to allow the employee to keep his title and salary but to diminish his responsibilities. Some personnel are difficult to remove not only because of the labour laws but also because they enjoy a close relationship with a person of influence.

NATIONALISM IN THE OFFICE

Indonesia was exploited by foreigners for over 300 years. She attained independence after an intense struggle and is aware of her youth as a nation as well as of her power in international situations.

It is very much the government's intent to foster nationalism in every citizen in every setting. It has been observed that Indonesia is trying to find the balance between nationalistic aspirations and economic development. The businessman will remember that learning to use the language, respecting the flag and the currency are interpreted as honouring the Indonesian national posture.

ATTITUDES TOWARD BUSINESS

Suku-isma: Among some ethnic groups—the Bataks and Minahasa particularly—the attitude of *suku-isma* or favouring the employment of their own people is very strong.

The Sophisticated Group: Professor Selo Soemardjan classified Indonesian businessmen into two groups. The first, the Sophisticated Group, is small numerically, urban, well and formally educated, in frequent contact with foreign officials, and its members understand both the material aspects and philosophy of western living.

They are also predominantly older men, many of whom were educated in the elite Dutch schools. They are widely regarded as bicultural, with an understanding, appreciation and integration of several world views or philosophies. They tend to be intensely nationalistic but liberal toward contracts, economic value of time, and the function of capital in public and private life. They are comfortable with their cultural values and can separate them from international business.

The Marginal Group: Membership of this group is perhaps ten times the size of the Sophisticated Group. These people are also urban, with formal but perhaps 'unpolished' education. Some have received training and advanced degrees abroad; others did not complete formal training. Their attachment to Indonesian culture can be superficial. Their outlook tends to be more rigid and conservative than that of the Sophisticated Group.

Marginals aspire to the material comforts of the foreigner but usually fail to appreciate the philosophy and work ethic that provide it. R.M. Hadjiwibowo, an Indonesian businessman, commented on the attitudes of the *priyayi* or civil servants (who belong to the Marginal Group) to a gathering of international businessmen: '... he is less interested in whether the end result is commensurate with the work expended. In a way he would similarly not be interested in the acquired skill after a course, but only in the certificate.'

Professor Soemardjan commented: 'Within this group a contract can become an instrument of impulse or a means to an end rather than a manifestation of mutual confidence. A casual attitude toward bad cheques or any other expeditious method to gain money (or) to conclude a business deal gains them neither the respect of the Indonesian nor the foreign community.'

The third and largest group comprises the rest of the population. They respect western ways of living and doing business but do not understand them. They are firmly members of their original culture and this dictates all their responses and values.

A Contrast of Systems

Professor Soemardjan presents a tidy contrast between the cultural elements of western capitalism and the 'village' cultural elements that affect Indonesian business. Western capitalism stresses individualism (both to excel and produce), liberal democracy, achievement orientation, science and technology, organisation of human skills, and rational and realistic reasoning motivated by profit-making. Contrasting with this is the strong *suku* ethic which values communality (of work and ownership), tradition-oriented democracy, achievement orientation with social obligations (to share and care), and a low level of science and technology. Manpower is organised primarily for social purposes and only secondarily for production objectives.

THE VIEW OF CONTEMPORARY RESEARCH

Indonesians have found their emerging national personality an object of interest and study. Dr Koentjaraningrat, a noted Indonesian anthropologist, described six common traits affecting the work ethic found among Indonesians following the prolonged post-revolutionary period (roughly 1949–60). It is worthwhile to compare these with Professor Soemardjan's description of the village value systems. The frame of reference for these remarks is as comparisons with the western work ethic. The six common traits are:

1. The tendency to neglect work quality.
2. Unwillingness to start a career 'from scratch'. In business or education projects the need is felt for a quick yield, immediate progress or direct advancement. This is compatible with Professor Selo Soemardjan's observation about the attitudes of the 'Marginal Group' of Indonesian businessmen.
3. An inferiority complex.
4. Undisciplined attitudes. This is most apparent in the areas of punctuality, long lunches, etc. and a reluctance to feel a sense of 'deadline' urgency regarding projects.
5. Reluctance to take responsibility. There is a tendency to shift personal responsibility with 'I was just following orders.'
6. Fondness for copying another's initiatives.

Dr Geert Hofstede, author of *Culture's Consequences*, produced a manual for TG International, Management Consultants in Jakarta in 1982. The booklet, 'Cultural Pitfalls for Dutch Expatriates in Indonesia', addresses itself to issues that face all expatriates, and lists 12 limitations to transferability of Dutch (or western) management methods:

1. Personal selection should take ethnic and family factors into account. It is important to understand the impact—both positive and negative—of *suku-isma* and the ethnic stereotypes when recruiting staff. There is also sensitivity about Indonesian Chinese and people of mixed Dutch-Indonesian parentage. 'In addition,' remarked an Indonesian businessman, 'Indonesia is a country of conformity. If you stand out you are the object of talk, teasing and social pressure. There is an attempt of other ethnic groups to conform and achieve a balance of non-domination.'

2. Payment by results is rarely possible. The relationship between employer and employee in Indonesia is perceived as a moral one. The employee expects to be rewarded for loyalty and seniority and not necessarily for performance.

3. Direct appraisal of performance is delicate.

4. Dismissal of employees is culturally undesirable. Poor performance is no reason for dismissal, but it may be a reason for an assignment to a different task.

5. Methods for management development should avoid direct confrontation. Interactions dear to the western heart— 'feedback', 'sensitivity training' and 'group discussion'—are likely to be met with silence by members of the middle management.

   An Indonesian businessman notes that most of the higher level managers have been trained in the west and are comfortable with contemporary western management techniques. The individual in middle management perceives these techniques as imported and not related to the situation in the office.

6. Go-betweens have an important role.

7. From time to time, *gotong-royong* (community labour) can be called for, but with care. The concept of shared community labour is being diluted and lost, according to some sociologists.

8. Models of participative management are out of place. The

Indonesian subordinate expects the superior to behave in an authoritarian manner.

9. Status differences are desirable. The Indonesians emphatically do not want the boss to be 'one of the guys'.

10. Formal politeness and the restraint of emotions are imperative. Distance of manner is maintained even in informal settings.

11. Punctuality and technical precision demand a lengthy learning process.

12. Sympathy for the weak should not be expected. In the west, social sympathy is a valued ethic and inspires many to work in technical and social aid fields. As Dr Hofstede observed, in Indonesia, it is customary to help only the poor within the family or village community.

THE EXPATRIATE VIEW

Some of the concerns (which may continue to affect his attitude and efficiency here) that the expatriate businessman, technician or expert must deal with before he decides to work in Indonesia are:

1. After a period served in an international situation, can you expect a better career choice to be available to you upon your return to your home company?

2. Some employment, for example in the international oil community, is by definition only available overseas. Is it possible that your decision to come to Indonesia was not personal choice but rather availability of work?

3. Are you here in a corporate position or as an independent? Do you have the support of a parent company?

4. Is your work situation primarily with other expatriates, only with nationals, or is the work force mixed?

5. How much did you know about the job before you arrived? Was the information correct? Fair? Complete?

6. Are you satisfied with your ability to provide for your family?

7. Does this move have the support of your family?

Another group who has made the decision to live and work abroad includes members of the foreign service, diplomats, United Nations personnel, international aid experts, teachers and missionaries. Many of these see working overseas as the obvious choice. This is often the group that makes the best personal adjustments.

What criticisms do expatriates have about the 'style' of their fellow businessmen?

1. Arrogance of manner in speaking, tone of voice, and a sense of personal superiority.
2. Lack of interest in the nationals, manifested in brusqueness, impersonality, and haste in business dealings.

Vocabulary

Corruption: By any definition, this is discouraged by the Indonesian government. People talk about it in vague, third-person terms. The following suggestions have been made: 'The definition of corruption is how the money is spent,' or 'Leave it alone and don't get involved. What you don't see, isn't there.'

Sogok, an old Javanese word absorbed by Bahasa Indonesia, refers to money 'under the table' to buy a place for a child in school or elicit preferences, for example. *Sogok* has been a part of normal business here for a long time, often in the form of a small gift for service rendered. *Pungli* is an abbreviation of *pungutan liar* which became popular in the 1980s. It describes unauthorised assessments/payments. Anti-corruption campaigns usually refer to *pungli*. *Korupsi* is an Anglicised word which means corruption in its contemporary, raw sense.

Indonesianisation: This describes the government programme whereby Indonesians assume jobs previously held by expatriates.

To feel ... to think: Most western languages translate the concept of 'I think ...' just like that. Expatriates learn that 'to think' in

Bahasa Indonesia is *pikir*. That really means 'to have an opinion, an idea or a thought'. The word that gives the best mileage and most pleases Indonesians is *rasa* which means 'to feel'—as in 'I have a feeling' or 'What if we ...' Start listening to the talk around you. Feel first, then think!

***PT, CT* and *Yayasan*:** The types of Indonesian companies that most expatriates will come in contact with are the *PT* or limited liability, and the *CV* or limited partnership where there is usually a silent partner who is only liable to the extent of his contribution to the capital of the company. In addition to these there are many government cooperatives and *Yayasan* which are a form of charitable institution.

The middlemen, facilitators who are used in business negotiations, are also instrumental in setting up (at high levels) many of the *PT* and *CV* companies. They often expect to receive a certain equity in the company in lieu of pay for their service.

Thank you: It is important to remember that Indonesians usually smile or nod in acknowledgement in situations where the westerner would say 'Thank you.' In a business sense, effusive thanks would be very difficult for the traditional Indonesian to accept without demurring to try to avoid the appearance of self-aggrandisement.

Transfer of Technology
This is what the government expects of every expatriate who comes to work in Indonesia. While the expatriate is treated as a guest and an expert, he is expected to teach and transfer his technical and management skills to the Indonesians.

One expatriate engineer remarked wistfully, 'If I do well here, I will work myself out of a job.'

Chapter Ten

CULTURE SHOCK

TRAVELLERS' ILLNESSES

There are three major illnesses that afflict the travellers of the world. The first two, jet-lag and traveller's tummy, are so commonplace that people rarely get in a twist about them. The red, dark-ringed eyes and weird sleep patterns of jet-lag are well understood and the associated behaviour—short temper, dullness, irritability and fatigue—is forgiven.

Those afflicted with traveller's tummy discuss the condition of their bowels with strangers or fellow travellers. They can usually count on receiving sympathy and understanding.

However, the third 'illness', culture shock, is an affliction of the feelings. Its visible aspects—weeping, confusion, anger, fear, frustration, acting-out or retreat—are not reactions to cherish.

Culture Shock Examined

Within the last 20 years, culture shock has been recognised and its manifestations studied. Dr Kalervo Oberg, an anthropologist associated with the United States Agency for International Development, observed culture shock at length, and established and named its various phases.

He called the initial stage of adjustment the honeymoon when all is perceived as wonderful. The second stage is when one feels the urge to function realistically. Fantasy does not work and the person becomes aggressive toward what he encounters in the host country. The third stage is a time of compromise and accommodation, and the fourth is the level of adjustment that each individual reaches.

I'm Not Shocked, I'm Confused

Most of us underestimate the degree to which we are products of our individual cultures. A person entrenched in his own cultural values is likely to view those that differ as 'quaint, interesting, or charming'. What he really means is 'different' and in extreme situations, 'wrong'.

Distress arises when 'quaint' becomes 'inconvenient' or 'unworkable', when 'interesting' becomes 'frustrating', and when 'charming' becomes 'confusing'. When an individual encounters an abundance of confusion that can be felt but not always seen and rarely understood, and his normal (cultural) way of coping with it will not work, he is dealing with culture shock.

Prove It!

Culture shock describes an all-pervading feeling of discomfort in your environment. All your familiar cues and props for taking care of yourself and getting along with others do not fit, are not effective, or threaten to embarrass you. An article, 'A Behavioural Analysis of Culture Learning' by G.M. Guthrie, points out five significant factors regarding learning to function in a second culture.

1. One's first culture understanding is acquired early, and is usually fixed by age five.

Think back to the manners learnt by age five or six. You had learnt to greet elders and peers 'correctly' and use 'good' manners at the table. If Asian, chopsticks or hands are correct; if western, a knife, fork and spoon are right. You had been taught acceptable ways to deal with anger. If western you learnt it was all right to express anger and hurt. If Javanese, you might be taught to suppress that. You learnt the priorities for your loyalties. A westerner would emphatically 'look out for Number One (himself!)' while the Asian would endeavour to become a part of the group.

Each of us is a product of our first culture. Some people become so controlled by it that they are unable to acknowledge, let alone accept, people and behaviour from other cultures. This condition is ethnocentrism. It means 'My way is the only way.' People limited by an ethnocentric point of view are likely to make these comments:
- If they knew better (my way!) they would change.
- This would never happen in my country!
- Smart people (like me) would never do that!
- Poor things, they don't know any different (my way).

2. New culture patterns are learnt more easily by children than by adults.

Children rely on visual cues. Acceptable behaviour is copied. The child in any culture has the constant reassurance that specific behaviour elicits predictable and positive results.

3. One's first culture determines habits of valuing.

What is valued in your culture? A sense of individuality? personal physical strength? self-reliance? high personal achievement? distance and restraint in human relations? aggression in business or a communal sense of ownership? sequential thinking? non-judgementalness? loyalty to family? to the political state? to religion?

All your first culture values will either assist or hinder you in functioning in a different culture. No matter how highly motivated we are to be accepting, initially all of us will interpret every situation in the light of our first culture values.

4. One's first culture introduces errors in interpretation of the second culture.

Now we have arrived at the moments of emotional chap. What we experience in one setting is felt differently by our emotions and intellect in another that appears similar.

We are taught to respond to tragedy with a long face and outpourings of concern. We are also taught that it is all right to feel bad when reporting a disaster.

Without being educated to understand the Javanese need to lighten the delivery of bad news with a deprecating laugh or gentle smile, the expatriate finds himself in a confusing situation. The cues he needs for an appropriate (first culture) response to bad news—long faces, tears, intense emotion—are replaced by laughter and light smiles which are his (first culture) cues for pleasure.

5. One can express best his deepest values in behaviour patterns that are of long standing.

As adults, our first language of 'feelings' and social responses is the cultural one with which we were raised. Y. Sugihara, in an unpublished Master's thesis at California State University, stated that the cross-cultural visitor or temporary resident in the new environment generally behaves as he did in his home country, although he may not be aware of it. Thus, there are times that he and the national host may not agree on appropriate behaviour.

There are numerous examples of this in the international business world in Indonesia. The foreign businessmen tend to be task-oriented; the Indonesian businessmen tend to value the personal relationship more than the task or the product. Foreigners fly into a frothing frenzy when deadlines for delivery of goods are not met; Indonesian shopkeepers expect understanding for the delays—sickness, time off for holidays, relatives visiting, etc.

Recreating Your Own Culture

Members of a minority culture will always seek each other for emotional support (not to be confused with friendship) which is related to keeping one's self-image intact. This is done by the creation and support of mini-national enclaves—clubhouses, sports clubs, the enthusiastic celebration of national days, and the availability of national foods in specialty shops or through embassies.

In the course of bicultural adjustment, many expatriates find this sort of socialising essential. For some, this attachment may remain strong for the duration of their posting overseas. Others may use it for a short time in the process of establishing new, independent relationships.

East and West Didn't Meet for Kipling

Will they meet for me? Yes. R. Taft remarked in 'Coping with Unfamiliar Cultures' (*Studies in Cross-Cultural Psychology*) that 'It is possible to be bicultural just as it is to be bilingual. Like the bilingual, a true bicultural (person) has the skills to perform competently the roles required by each cultural context and he is able to avoid gaffes that could result from inappropriate switching between cultures.'

Sometimes these manifestations of biculturalism are situational. For example, Indonesians willingly confess that when they drive in Europe or the United States they are comfortable with the controlled traffic. As soon as they return to Indonesia, they adapt to the less disciplined traffic patterns. Foreigners have been heard to remark as they managed a U-turn across a traffic median, 'I would never do this at home.' A recent traveller observed that a group of Indonesians queued quietly to board a plane from Perth to Jakarta. When the wheels touched down on arrival, there was the familiar and acceptable scramble for hand luggage and crush to reach the exit. This behaviour would have been unacceptable in Australia four hours before.

How Do You Think?

It isn't really so much '*What* do you think?' as '*How* do you think?' Indonesian scholars and students of human behaviour have commented on the approaches to thinking of the typical westerner and the Indonesian. They make the following comparison.

The typical westerner is a linear thinker. He begins at one position and moves logically through the data, looking for patterns. The western mind is bound by all sorts of logical criteria. It has the security that what is defined is all right. The thinker in the west tends to consider those who do not accept the beautiful logic of this as stupid, ignorant, dumb …

The Indonesian views the problem to be solved as one that is constantly changing and needing re-interpretation. He tends to see things in terms of relationships and feelings. He is aware of constantly shifting boundaries to the situation. He is extremely sensitive to another's intent. The most important criterion is whether another is moving toward or away from the current group goal or consensus. The Indonesian tends to consider those who do not accept the beautiful logic of this as insensitive, unsophisticated, concerned with quick material accomplishments …

CULTURE SHOCK SCHEDULE

During the first six months most people establish patterns for their adjustment. While none of us has the luxury of precisely 'scheduling' reactions and attitudes, the following seems generally apt.

These descriptions of activities and behaviour during the settling in period have been drawn from the experiences of many expatriates, articles in magazines and books, and discussions with members of the international business community.

Pre-Departure

'I'm so excited!'

Activities: Aptly described as planning, packing, processing, partying and parting.

Attitudes: Anticipation of new things and a lessening of interest in current responsibilities.

Emotions: Enthusiasm and excitement. There is general family concern about leaving friends, relatives and the familiar environment. This is especially felt by children, but they are rarely able to interpret their feelings.

Physical responses: Fatigue, a tendency to run on nervous energy and sometimes psychosomatic illness (if the person is ambivalent about the move).

The First Month

'It's wonderful! Even the palms have a rosy glow!'

Activities: Welcome. VIP or special treatment. Sheltered care in a hotel. Abundance of newness—the office, colleagues, house, foods, sights, sounds, responsibilities.

Attitudes: Curiosity about the nationals, the country, the culture. Tendency to downplay negative feelings about the local situation. Everyone is friendly! It's great.

Emotions: Sense of mission. You have included your aspirations, hopes and expectations in the luggage. You are a tourist, an explorer. Euphoria!

Physical responses: Sleeplessness, mild stomach upsets, trouble with the heat, low energy.

The Second Month

'What happened to paradise?'

Activities: Ambivalent about undertaking formal language training or relying on a phrasebook. Moving from the 'shelter' of a hotel into a house. Full job responsibilities. Possible frustration about the shipment. You begin to see and smell unpleasant things. The awareness arrives that not everything is cheap! You begin to confront the reality of local transportation systems and traffic.

Attitudes: Neutral toward environment … just another day in paradise. Skeptical … the shipment may arrive with the next Ice Age! Realisation that your own and others' values are different. 'I can't bathe without hot water. Fix the heater now!' You begin criticising, judging, comparing. 'Even dead flies on window sills got painted!'

Emotions: Nervous. Uncertain about how to function. Restless. The search for security (friends, national group, familiar foods and activities) begins. 'I'd sell my soul for a Big Mac!' At the same time there may be the beginning of emotional withdrawal and retreat from the scene. 'I can't face another day in the traffic.'

Physical responses: Colds, headaches, tropical lassitude, vague illnesses often defined by hour (12-hour bug, 24-hour glup, etc.). Compulsive tendency to inform the world that you have diarrhoea—just in case it is really a symptom of a rare and fatal tropical disease.

The Third Month

'Can I exchange for another country in my size and colour, please?'

Activities: Language study may stop. (The usual excuse being you are too busy with office work or setting up home.) Tendency to cling to own cultural group. Work performance and efficiency may be patchy (refers to businessmen, housewives and schoolchildren).

Attitudes: Discouraged, irritable, hypercritical. Withdrawal from contact with Indonesians. 'I want to be alone.' Introspective. Fear of theft, bodily harm, injury, cheating, contamination. 'How do I know I'm not being ripped off?' You develop the 'tropical stare'. You

begin to collect, accept and utilise negative stereotypes.
Emotions: Discouraged, 'bummed out'. Friends aren't wonderful. No one wants to hear the list of gripes again. Suspicious of servants. Over-concern about sanitation. 'Is it possible to boil the air?'
Physical responses: General feeling of illness. Time lost from the job. Extreme fatigue. Wistful ponderings of vacations, end of term.

The Fourth Month

'I still don't like it and I want to go home ... maybe.'
The third month drags into the fourth with gradual positive adjustments. There is a renewal of interest and energy often associated with growing familiarity with the language, success in establishing friendships, competence in the market—a feeling of satisfaction with accomplishments. 'Guess what I found in the market yesterday?'

The Fifth Month

'I'm settled! Come on! I'll show you around.'
Activities: May resume language study. 'It's much easier now that I speak a little of the language.' Work improves. Routine established, goals set and plans made to achieve projects. 'We're planning a family trip to Lake Toba.'
Attitudes: Constructive, positive outlook. Skills of compromise and accommodation developed. 'Everyone's different. Find what works for you.'
Emotions: Increased interest in the surroundings and the job. Or, if the adjustment is not successful, the feeling is 'Bag it! ... and flee.'
Physical responses: Normal.

The Sixth Month to End of Term

'Welcome to our home!'
Activities: The established routine is supportive and fulfilling. There are generally pleasant interruptions of travel and special events. 'There's a big ceremony in Bali next month. Let's all go!' As the

job finishes, there is reduced interest in things local and a projection for things to come—see 'The First Month' and 'Pre-Departure'.

Attitudes: Generally maintained on a plateau.

Emotions: Both pleasure and pain are perceived as real and relatively stress-free. 'Oh, it's just one of those days! The squirrel got her teeth trapped in the rag she sleeps in, the cook has a cold and I don't want her sneezing into the salad and someone forgot to wind the clock so I thought it was 10 all day!' Most people have worked out compromises to problems. 'I don't care if the servants fold the bath towels like origami figures, as long as they are clean!'

Physical responses: Health tends to be stable.

Moving Out

'Moving right along!'

Activities: Interest in local affairs lessens. Disengagement and anticipation of the next job/transfer/country begins.

Attitudes: This can be either a neutral or a high production phase. Some people feel they must finish everything that was ever begun, buy everything in the market, or see every sight in the country. 'I've got my things ordered to go in the shipment.'

Emotions: Planning for the move, turning over the job, decrease in production, a 'lame duck', 'short-timer' mentality.

Physical responses: Generally all right.

MAKING FRIENDS

The culture shock schedule reassures that generally at one time or other, and for varying periods of time, those are the feelings and attitudes we all deal with. That is the good news. Having arrived at the sixth month, few achieve Buddha-like serenity and rise above the scene. Life must be lived daily and there are moments, hopefully graced with laughter, when each person sags into relapse. That is the bad news. However, there is the assurance, founded in experience, that the dreadful moments are shorter and easier to deal with.

Will You Be My Friend?

Nothing can replace a friendship that grows through years of shared experiences. Especially for women, living overseas may be the first time you have consciously had to think about making friends.

In a foreign environment, this process is accelerated. Each of us is eager to change our status from stranger to friend. Often, the first and best friends are the people you meet as arrivals in the hotel. Together you go through the process of coping with similar problems and frustrations, ultimately settling in. As satisfying as these friendships are for companionship, they do not always expand the arrival's experience and skills for living in this new place.

Later, the office, the school, your national group and your church are sources of friends. Many of these groups have special programmes for newcomers. Go as part of a group or go alone. You may have to make the effort to reach out for friendship.

The Survival List

As you begin to establish your life here, provide yourself with necessary information so that you can function knowledgeably.

1. Get a good map of your city and mark important areas—the office, your home, shopping areas.
2. Know the name (and be able to pronounce it), the address, and the phone number of the office.
3. Know your address and how to say it. Sometimes the driver knows the house, but the newcomer does not.

    There have been incidences where newcomers were making small talk and got to the point of exchanging address and phone numbers. Women have been first embarrassed, then frustrated, and finally in tears because they did not know their address ... and had to dig in their purse for the scrap of paper that would get them home.
4. Have name cards printed. They are inexpensive and commonly used.

Back to the Task of Making Friends

Sign up to be on a committee for a project that looks interesting. If it is a bore, what have you lost? Usually nothing. You are out of the house, meeting people and gathering your impressions of life here.

Your tendency will be to announce that you have just arrived. That provokes predictable responses in your companions. The positive one is likely to be an effusive, sincere WELCOME! (Also be prepared in a superficial social setting to hear claims of happiness and what you probably perceive correctly to be a 'show' of contentment. This does not imply that the people are masking feelings of deep despair; it is simply new acquaintances exchanging tentative remarks.)

The negative response is likely to be a recital of humourless complaints. You must set the tone of the conversation. How?

Learn to Complain Charmingly

Be assertive about meeting people. Tell what you have done, what you like to do, what your skills are, and ask questions that convey your interest in your new situation here.

Be honest with yourself and others about your feelings and observations. This is important and equally an exercise in self-discipline. Honesty in reporting feelings is not to be equated with a license to complain and carp.

Learn to deliver the 'I' statement. This allows you to register your personal feelings without casting blame or pinning responsibility outside yourself. Here are some examples:

- I really feel the heat. I plan my excursions carefully so I can get cool quickly if necessary. (Compare with: This country's weather is just so hot that I can't get a thing done.)
- I miss my family at home. It helps to call regularly. I am grateful for the International Direct Dial system. (Compare with: Do you realise it took over a month to get a letter from home? What's the matter with the mail here?)

- I appreciate the help with the housework but I need time alone in the house. Most of the work gets done in the morning, so I look forward to quiet afternoons. (Compare with: Every time I open a door, there's someone there! Don't the maids know when I want to be alone?)

Periodically, each of us needs to roar ungraciously and vent frustrations. The key is to discipline yourself to expose your foul mood ONCE to a trusted friend and then consider the moment past. For the rest of the day a casual 'I'm having a bad day,' delivered with no details, allows you to indicate your feelings and frees those around you to continue their activities, unencumbered by your bad mood.

The Negative Comment

Maintaining your mental equilibrium in the face of some of the frustrations outside of your own culture is a full-time job. All the best intentions in the world get chapped when the electricity fails, the house appears to fall apart, or personal problems—yours and others'—refuse reasonable solutions.

The consistently negative person is ultimately avoided. 'I smile, nod and walk away—fast,' remarked one woman. 'Who wants to hear all that?' queried a businessman.

Few can withstand a repeated assault on their carefully constructed positive state of mind. Equally few wish to be reminded of the pain and confusion they may have experienced when they first arrived. (Some remark lightly that they have no memory of the first six months.)

Few adults will try to talk to another adult into understanding or happiness. Therefore, for the newcomer who genuinely feels confusion, distress and frustration, the challenge becomes finding out how to express this in an acceptable way. Refer to the 'I' messages (page 211) and practise them.

The Long-Stayer

The long-stayer (over two years) can be a source of emotional support and basic information for the newcomer. The special challenge for the long-stayer is to maintain the energy to make new friends as old ones leave. 'I am so tired of standing on the tarmac and waving goodbye to friends,' sighed one after the Spring exodus.

While the newcomer is fascinated and absorbed by his or her perceptions, the long-stayer goes through the steps of 'How long have you been here? Where are you living? Do you have children? What are your interests? Where have you lived before?' to finally arrive at the friendly golf date or luncheon invitation.

The long-stayer also runs the risk of becoming every newcomer's Yellow Pages. One long-time resident reported that in a social chat it was indicated that she had been in Indonesia for a lengthy period. The conversation changed at once into an account of the other's daughter's ankle socks that did not get packed in the shipment and where-in-the-world could more be got? The information was given, the socks purchased, and another small problem solved.

No one begrudges this sort of shoppers' service relationship. Rarely do expatriates meet without a breathless exchange of 'I saw cranberry sauce at ...' or 'The sports shop near the theatre has good track suits at a fair price ...' or 'The dates are in from Saudi Arabia for Lebaran ...'

This exercise usually includes listing and comparing of current prices. Many expatriates report being baffled or put off by everyone's need to know what something cost. In many cultures in the west that would be considered bad manners; here it is polite conversation.

The average stay of most expatriates working in Indonesia is 2–3 years, just about the period of time that the psychologists suggest it takes to really settle in. However, most expatriates work hard at maintaining their international friendships with steady correspondence, visits on holidays, and being available to entertain friends of friends.

SETTLING IN

Viewed as an individual challenge, dealing with your own temporarily sulphurous moods is probably possible. However, the situation compounds itself as the family tries to settle in.

Little Children

You cannot take a child out of a packing box and place him prettily on the new bed. Children, from infants to teenagers, are working through their adjustments, too. They are not fooled with the promise of newness, large rooms and swimming pools. They are pragmatists.

Nancy Piet-Pelon, a professional in family planning who worked many years in Jakarta and Southeast Asia, wrote and spoke frequently on the subject of adjustment of families overseas. She indicated the following areas of awareness for parents of young children.

1. Children and their relationship with the 'changed' you (and the changed environment)

Children look to their parents for support and answers. If the child is too young to have been included in discussions about the move, be prepared to discuss why you are here. This is especially important if the child equates being *here* with being taken away from *there*, which was safe and understood. Be prepared to answer questions about the country. Your ability to respond to your child's curiosity and concerns will be reassuring.

Children have to try to fit into a new school with people who might not look or sound the same as themselves. Friendship groups at school form quickly and newcomers can be excluded. Going to a friend's house to play often requires elaborate transportation arrangements, with mothers or servants in the car. For children who came from small towns or cozy neighbourhoods, this can be a real change. For mothers used to driving children to dancing lessons, club meetings and a friend's house to play, having a responsible driver to do this can be a real relief.

2. Children and their relationship with servants

Your breezy 'Here, Anik will take care of you' may only convince your child that he is being given away or at least taken out of your care. You will want to assume a concerned responsibility toward your child's view of the caretaker or *babu anak*.

Most children enjoy a relationship of affection and trust with the domestic staff. It is important to realise that Indonesian methods of 'socialising' a youngster are in many ways different from those in the west. Indonesian children can do almost no wrong; they are protected, and their behaviour excused, rationalised and accepted. Unacceptable behaviour is dealt with in a placating manner, with food, promises of toys or diversions. The reverse is threatening with ghosts. Indonesians use these techniques to deal with their child or yours.

3. Children's ways of dealing with negative situations

The very situations that seem the most normal to a young child can quickly become negative. Consider the following example: the act of drinking water from the tap and taking fruit from the kitchen table is now surrounded by warnings about worms and germs and things that will make him sick. Typical response: irrational fears about food and regression with toilet habits.

Naps and bedtime might be associated with times that the child is left with caretakers. Typical response: irrational fears and dreadful scenes associated with bedtime and sleeping.

The child who is just coming to grips with his own language may discover that the additional people in the house cannot understand him. What's worse, his parents may speak the different language too, which adds to his confusion. One young child communicated her desire for jam and tomato sandwiches. She received one jam-and-tomato sandwich—and the firm conviction that she had said something wrong! Typical response: sullenness, withdrawn and shy behaviour.

Children are quick to learn that a servant rarely says 'no'. One mother returned to see her toddler playing with a very sharp kitchen knife. Her question, 'Why did you give him the knife?' brought this response which was reasonable from the maid's point of view, '*Dia mahu.*' (He wanted it.)

The food does not look, taste or smell right to many small children. They may be pressed to eat strange foods to please strangers. Typical response: more irrational fear of food, petulance and insistence on certain limited foods, throwing up.

What Should You Do?

Children also need a great deal of reassurance and security. The mother of small children should spend time getting them settled rather than worry about setting up the home.

Keep your own culture alive. Bedtime stories, family holidays and family rituals need to be observed as long as they are important to the family. Some families invent special events that are anticipated and of value to them.

Keep photograph albums of relatives and family events. Set up your communication system with distant friends—cassette tapes may be exchanged or regular telephone calls arranged.

Many expatriate families have been lucky in finding older couples who will function as 'surrogate grandparents' for their children. This can be a rich experience for everyone concerned.

Pre-teen Children

If you are going to live in a remote location, plan for your children's education long before you leave home. There are a number of international schools scattered about the country. Jakarta has the greatest number and the largest. These are without boarding facilities.

To provide the opportunities for socialising so important to pre-teens and teens, many families opt for boarding a child rather than the relatively solitary situation of correspondence courses.

Teens

Both formal research and the instincts of parents suggest that it is difficult to move teens away from familiar settings during the high school years. Some teens respond to the need to stay with known peers and may choose a boarding school.

For teens who join their family overseas some situations to be dealt with are:

1. They need to find their place in a school and with a peer group.
2. In Indonesia it is difficult for the teen to find satisfying part-time or holiday work.
3. The teens' access to the car, and freedom to drive that is common in the west, may be curtailed.
4. They may resent their high visibility in the foreign community. Teens, who are especially absorbed by developing and testing their own individuality, may find the pressures of being 'a guest in the country' or 'a representative of their own country' or 'aware of their father's position' difficult to deal with.
5. If the adjustment is difficult, the family may consider an alternative plan—perhaps sending teens home or to a boarding school.

The Husband or Father

His reasons for working overseas are varied: a career; an opportunity for additional training and experience that will lead to advancement; the only available employment.

We are familiar with situations where members of the family resist the common experience of being seen as representatives of the father's company, country, or position. They resent being viewed by host country nationals as national stereotypes with the consequent sense of loss of individuality. Often the distress felt by the family members is directed to the father: '… whose work brought us here!'

Second, studies in some overseas schools indicate that teenagers often put their own interpretation on the endless work and social activities of parents. Arriving in Indonesia, most men are met on the job with a list of things to do! Parents should differentiate between what is done for personal pleasure and for social reasons.

If the father is seen as an extension of his work, according to the studies, his role diminishes in an expatriate domestic setting. There he is viewed as a distant figure in the family constellation who makes the important family decisions, establishes high expectations for the family, but in most cases is not sought out as a confidante.

The Mother or Wife

Most women assume the responsibility of providing emotional balance in the home. They function as attitude setter, soother, explainer, facilitator, cook, decorator, transportation manager, social secretary, and nurse/doctor. To direct your energy in a positive and focused way, examine priorities. Just for this day, what is the order of importance? It can change from day to day. Here is a sample list:
1. Order and routine in the home.
2. Personal space and privacy.
3. A satisfying social life.
4. The pursuit of new skills.
5. A recognised role in the family.

Setting up the home

The newly arrived wife almost always sees establishing the home as her first priority, creating a haven where the family feels secure and can be themselves, with as nearly as possible the look, smell, routine, ritual, food and security the family enjoyed before the transfer overseas. To delay would only increase her anxiety.

There are two considerations to note here. The first is that the emotional needs of children may have to take precedence over ordering curtains and looking at furniture. The second is that many wives feel that their ability to care for their family is synonymous with unpacking and decorating.

Several things will conspire against you in this regard. If shopkeepers sense that you are tense with urgency to obtain goods and services, they will promise delivery an hour ago—just to make you happy. The frustrations mount as days go by and no curtains, no furniture, no repairmen arrive.

'My husband is at the office, the kids are in school, and I'm in Indonesia!' laments the flustered wife. It is she who will come into most contact with the Indonesians. She needs the assistance of shopkeepers, servants, repairmen. To get it requires unusual skill with the language, knowledge of the shops, awareness of prices and work schedules—skills she has yet to learn.

Mother, M.D.

The mother is expected to attend to the physical health of the family. It is she who has to see that the water is boiled, the vegetables and fruits soaked and washed, the hands kept clean. She must achieve a balance between reasonable and irrational behaviour. She will reassure, for instance, that not every gas pain is a rupturing appendix, not every fever a malarial attack, and that anyone anywhere can get worms.

Women and work

The opportunity for work for dependent wives in Indonesia is limited. It would be a major error to assume satisfactory work will appear. The woman who is interested in promoting her career, or who needs to work to meet a family financial plan, or is considering leaving an active professional career at home should give deep thought to the consequences of moving to Indonesia. These needs are not likely to be met here.

Quality time

Here, society values women who spend their time in cultural pursuits, learning about Indonesia, and giving their time to charities

219

and welfare organisations. One woman observed, 'Most women who were aggressive about pursuing an interest or staying busy are full-time volunteers.'

Take it easy

Do not expect limitless understanding from your family or friends. Be easy on yourself. Take your time. Do not be intimidated by the fact that everyone else seems to be settled.

Separate your personal ability to get things done from the fact that the phone, the car, the traffic, and other cosmic glitches will conspire against you. You will learn to be patient with yourself and accepting of others.

Mother, business manager

Usually the wife becomes the executive director in the business of running her home. Her main job is to manage the domestic staff. She and her husband need to decide the areas of responsibility. The servants need to know who their boss is, and to understand the chain of command.

As in any business, women have discovered that some time spent at the same time each day—usually first thing in the morning—checking the status of the house, the chores to be done, and being visible to the servants will ensure a smooth operation. Establish your own routine. Here are some suggested techniques of organisation, in random order, that have been used successfully by expatriates in Indonesia.

1. *The telephone:* Decide how you want it answered and messages noted. Ensure a place for paper, pencils, a notebook and the phone directories. Do the servants inform you that you have had calls, or do you look in the notebook? Have a policy on how much information is given to strangers if you are out of the house. Establish a policy regarding the degree of access the servants have to the phone.

2. *Deliveries to the home:* Select a spot in the house where all letters, notes and small packages will be left to be picked up or delivered.

3. *Keeping accounts:* The kitchen 'Want List' is an assumed part of running any household. The expatriate wife and her staff will probably adjust quickly to the use of Bahasa Indonesia and her own language in the kitchen. Be prepared to train the staff to write the needs before you run out. Develop a filing system for recording deliveries of gas bottles, the pest control service, the monthly garbage collection. Decide if you want to keep a shopping record (this is helpful at first to learn the prices).

4. *The social calendar:* Consider keeping an appointments calendar for the cook/maid in which you can note down dinner parties and menus and indicate when you will be out. This can also inform the maid when to expect persons coming to the house.

5. *Keeping track of you:* Remember to tell your staff what your schedule is or where you will be. (Instruct them not to disclose that information to others.) It gives them the ability to find you if there is an urgent message or need at home. List and post crucial phone numbers of family contacts: children's friends, office numbers, doctor's office and others.

6. *Keeping track of servants:* The kitchen calendar is a good place to write down each servant's day off, time taken for classes or leave. Then the information is recorded impersonally and no one has to trust to memory.

SERVANTS

One of the biggest concerns for expatriates in Indonesia are servants and household management. It is possible that the arriving expatriate has never had experience with a full staff of servants, has mixed feelings about the situation, and feels at a loss.

Are servants really necessary? Yes. They are essential to accomplish the daily tasks that would have you hanging over a chair

221

and weeping at the end of a week. They are also essential from their point of view. They fit in with the communal, interlocked view of life. They are the architects of the graceful, leisurely lifestyle that exists here.

The Special Status of Servants

In Java you will encounter a culture which accommodates the server and the served. Scholars speculate that the cultural acceptance of serving is related to the centuries of influence of the Indian kingdoms. It is a fact that entire villages in Central Java are sources of servants. In the traditional setting, servants were attached to a family for generations. They were cared for as family. They often worked for very low wages but had the guarantee of total, lifetime care. Most servants in Java are Javanese. On other islands, among other ethnic groups, it is common to find persons who work for their affluent relatives in exchange for food, home, education and health care.

The average westerner does not employ servants in this capacity. Unable to provide the security of endless years of employment, he usually opts to pay a higher wage while still assuming the responsibility for lodging, food, clothes and health care during the term of employment.

Hiring Servants

The chances are potential staff will be lined up to be interviewed long before you leave the confines of the hotel or guest house. Rarely will you need to go looking: they find you. The larger cities may have some sort of employment service where prospective staff can be interviewed (usually in Bahasa Indonesia).

It is common for groups of servants to establish themselves in various foreign communities—diplomatic, oil, school—and hence to be aware of job vacancies and 'get the word out' to relatives and friends. In addition, many servants will keep tabs on the long-stayers in the community who will often act as intermediaries to recommend and place them.

Do not be pressured into hiring before you know your needs. Friends and colleagues are quick to tell you what you need, but only *you* will know, so take your time. Neither your house nor your life will fall apart in the time it takes you to make your decision.

If you need help with the language, ask someone to act as interpreter. It is crucial that all understand what is said. It is important to cover the following areas: wage, tasks, holidays or time off, clothing allowance, and health care. Most servants have a wad of reference letters. These are often more significant to the servant than they are reliable for the potential employer.

What Servants Expect

The minimum work conditions would include one day (24 hours) free per week, taken weekly or saved to be taken once a fortnight or once a month; two suits of clothes a year; health care (this includes dental and optical care, visits to the local doctor, hospitalisation and physical examinations); a week or ten days off at Lebaran or another holiday; the Lebaran bonus (a month's wage); and the agreed wage.

The wage

In traditional Indonesian life, the wage is considered separate from other money due or earned by the individual (i.e., rice, transportation and daily meal money). This wage or *gaji* is considered available to the entire family. The person who earned it may have no control over it. Indeed, to question the right of another's—usually an elder's—claim to the money would be considered rude and disrespectful. Therefore, if you ask where the salary went, the individual might tell you with absolute honesty, 'It is finished.'

The contemporary situation seems to be that until marriage, the young worker routinely remits most of the salary home. After marriage, he or she controls more of the money but it and they become the target for loans.

The demands on the wage are great—for school fees, medical expenses, wedding or burial money for other members of the family, the observance of specific life-cycle ceremonies, not to mention the relatively high cost of living such as the rice, the cooking oil, kerosene and clean water.

Borrowed money is safe

Money that is safe, the property of the individual, is money that has been borrowed for a specific purpose. One of the most efficacious ways for a servant to 'save' for anything is to borrow the money. Thus it is common for a new employee, basking in the security of a job, to immediately ask for a loan.

This need not be met with panic. The following anecdote is instructive. A wash girl received news that her child was ill in the village. She asked for leave to return and the loan of a month's salary. Rather than get angry or subject her to a lecture on the values of thrift (neither of which reactions she would understand), the *Nyonya* asked about the sick child. Was the sickness diagnosed? Had the child been taken to the doctor? Was it receiving care? The servant replied that she may be expected to buy medicine. The *Nyonya* replied that if she had money and did not after all need to spend it on medicine, the family in the village would put demands on it and she would return moneyless. The servant was relieved. She could now tell her family that her funds were limited, not by her lack of desire to provide, but by the decision of her *Nyonya*.

The employer has the option to refuse requests. However, everyone appreciates and respects efforts to work out a compromise. Your particular philosophy regarding loans is up to you. Make your rules clear. Keep careful, accurate written records. Be consistent and the servants will support and understand your policies. It may take a long time to repay the loan. The pay-back is a mere trickle because the wage is small. It is wise for the employer to consider the amount of time to pay it back rather than the amount of money!

The western view of money is to encourage individual control and thrift and to discourage debt. Accordingly, many expatriates try to set up savings accounts and thrift plans with or for their staff. The results seem to be mixed and reflect the sophistication and experience of individual servants.

Arranging the wage

Here, the gross amount is viewed in parts: the *gaji pojok* (base wage, which is often used for the needs of the entire family), borrowed money which remains under the discretion of the borrower, and those aspects of the total salary that are earmarked for basic needs—rice, daily meals, transportation, etc. Bonuses are usually based on the amount of the *gaji pojok* and not on the gross amount.

As the sophistication of the servants as a working class increases, more servants and employers are moving from the traditional *gaji pojok*/rice money arrangement to dealing with the wage as a lump sum item.

The Trial Period

When employment is offered to a servant, it is usually understood that the first month is a time to determine if the servant will fit in with the other household members. If at the end of the month all are satisfied, the wage is usually increased slightly, a physical check-up is arranged, the first suit of clothes is given and the deal is considered set.

The Tasks

It makes sense to assume at the outset that a gardener can cut grass and a wash girl can wash clothes. It is more helpful to make it clear that their primary responsibility is to make you happy. (Refer to '*Asal Bapak Senang*'.) Remembering their background of communal living and the need to fit in with (*cocok*) the rest of the group, consider emphasising that you want a harmonious group of workers (*rukun*) whose primary job it is to get along and to please you. That is a little hard for the egalitarian, task-oriented westerner to swallow.

However, the dividends come because the servants would have heard what makes sense to them. If there is trouble they understand the concept of not fitting in (*tidak cocok*) and would accept that as a reason for dismissal.

The Concept of Control

'Do-It-Yourself' could only be a popular concept in the west. The typical westerner associates 'control' with personal involvement. This is not the case here. Control is more a matter of delegation of task than of authority. The *Nyonya* and *Tuan* are expected to issue requests, and retain control and responsibility. (See the section on loans, page 224.)

Earning Your Pay

When a westerner accepts a job, it is normally for a specified number of hours per week. It is assumed that steam will rise from the labouring body, figuratively if not literally, for that time.

Servants in Indonesia are hired to serve, in labour and in attitude. They are blissfully untouched by a need to 'earn their pay' by working a non-stop 8–10 hour day. Your roar of rage when the gardener is having mid-morning tea or playing cards by the gate lights in the evening will fall on confused ears. Equally, when they have performed the requisite, regular jobs, unless you specify an unusual chore they will not normally look for additional work.

Helping Your Servants Handle Hassles

Your servants will act as 'filters' or interpreters for persons who might call on the telephone or appear, unsolicited, at your gate.

When a servant answers the phone, it is a good idea to give the impression that the house is occupied. Therefore, perhaps *Tuan* is napping, or having a bath. The person's name and number should be noted with a promise to return the call.

Any number of clever requests are used by unscrupulous persons to get inside the gate to 'case' your house or property. In general, people keep the gate locked and meet any guest at the gate, not inside.

Foreigners are advised to know who and where the local neighbourhood chairman, the *lurah*, is. It is this official's responsibility to give permission to people who are canvassing the neighbourhood for charity. You have the right to see the letter of permission from your *lurah*. You also have the right to call your company to ask if they have any record of persons working the neighbourhood. If the person is not bona fide, the threat of these two actions should discourage him.

One foreigner reports that a pair appeared at the gate recently, decked with 'official' documents. They announced that they were representatives of the city government and had arrived 'to spray the house and yard for cholera'. They were suggesting an astonishing service in view of the fact that cholera is spread by anal-oral faecal contamination. One wondered who or what they were going to spray. Or more accurately, whose what? In addition, they offered to collect today and spray tomorrow. Bargains like that are hard to pass up, but it is a good idea to try.

Usually, the servants can spot a phony, but are unwilling to be assertive about telling him to take a long walk in the traffic. If you take the lead, the servants will back you up, literally nodding agreement from a position behind you. Never get involved in one of these encounters alone.

Mini-Situations: A to Z

Dress: Servants regard themselves as workers with status. Looking well on the job is important to them. Older female servants usually wear traditional dress; older housemen or male cooks and drivers opt for a casual sort of uniform with a white suit for 'company'. Young girls prefer to work in nice day dresses. Gardeners will usually work in grubby clothes but will bathe and change if they have gate duty.

Accounts: All will welcome your guidelines for accountability. When errands are run, ask for receipts and an accounting. This way, you maintain control in the house.

Death: If a servant dies in your employ, usually a payment equal to two or three months' salary is expected by his family to defray the costs of burial and the socialising associated with the funeral.

Equality: Indonesians say of valued family servants, 'They are like our family.' You nod happily at this confirmation of equality. They add, 'We treat them as children.' Pop goes the egalitarian bubble! The expatriate employer is not here to change the social system. He is probably going to have more exposure to the servant class and the servant mentality than to any other group of Indonesians. It should be abundantly clear that all Indonesians are not like your servants. It is not neo-colonial, patronising, or paternalistic to recognise that the servants consider themselves a special class of workers. Their traditional world view is one of accepting one's lot in life and not aspiring to greater heights. Servants have secure jobs and receive a guaranteed wage, a condition they share with only 15 per cent of the population. It is appropriate and sensitive to their realistic needs to do for them what their culture allows them to expect.

Firing: The labour laws on servants seem to be established by tradition. Therefore, it is important to inquire from Indonesian colleagues and neighbours what is considered normal in your area. A servant will usually try to be fired rather than quit voluntarily because he is then, by common practice, entitled to an extra amount of money (usually an additional month's salary) from the employer. A servant who quits voluntarily will receive only the wages due him for the balance of the month.

Honesty: Most Indonesian servants are honest. This situation can be reinforced by making it clear
- who gets food scraps from the refrigerator;
- how the kitchen accounts will be handled;
- that you require receipts and accounting;
- that they do (or don't) have access to the coffee, tea and sugar;
- that you will (or won't) supervise gas and mileage on the car;
- that you will assume responsibility for caring for your money and jewellery.

Meritorious service: When you have had a large party or house guests, it is customary to give the servants additional money, roughly equivalent to a day's wage. Do not overdo it.

Pecking order: Servants will arrange themselves in some order of status that makes sense to them. It may be related to the ethnic backgrounds of the group, sex, age or experience. It is up to you to figure it out and to interact with it accordingly. Usually the driver considers himself apart from the domestic staff. The oldest servant or the cook is at the top of the group and the one who will most often express the concern of the others or bring problems for discussion.

Reading minds: You are regarded by your staff as incredibly wealthy, wise and powerful. They are grateful and relieved at indications that you understand their culture and behaviour.

Servants and the neighbourhood: Usually your servants will become friends with the other servants on the street and the people who keep the small stores. This is one of the ways in which you also become part of the neighbourhood scheme of things. Do not underestimate the importance of this relationship.

Servants' guests: The guest is an honoured person in any situation and all work stops in the effort to be hospitable. On your servants' day off—especially Sunday—you can expect their relatives and friends to *mampir* (drop in) for tea and light conversation with them. Present a patina of graciousness if you encounter these guests in the servants' quarters. That is not the time to issue requests for work. Wait until the guests leave.

Short memories: When you are dealing with money, days off, any sort of special arrangement, make an obvious show of writing it down. Then, if there is any confusion—'Who, me?'—everyone can talk about what is written, a neutral, face-saving situation.

Your job as teacher: If your observations of the work or work schedule suggest a change in the way things are done, it is better to teach by showing. Be prepared to repeat the process several times, each time as though it were the first!

A Final Word on Servants

If the relationship has gone from grand to grim, do not invest time in prolonging the misery. Experience suggests that it will not improve.

If you had made it clear at the outset that your primary work criterion was to make you, the boss, happy, then quickly and without indulging in wishful rationalisations, present the person with the money due to him, a letter confirming his terms of employment and announce that as he no longer fits (*tidak cocok*), he will be happier in another place. It is important not to get drawn into a discussion of specific grievances. Keep it simple, brief and non-personal.

Speak privately, not in front of the other staff or known friends, gently and with no show of anger. (Anger, personal remarks and accusations can lead to bad feelings, *malu*, and sometimes violence.)

If you are uncomfortable with this task, ask an Indonesian friend to witness the event. This would still be considered private.

SINGLES

Some specific situations face the 'singles' in Indonesia. Culturally, the Indonesians consider the single status a condition to change as soon as possible. Therefore, from the middle and servant classes you could expect some concerned queries—'Why are you not (yet) married?' Answers relating to your professional rather than personal life are received with scepticism.

Age and experience are given respect and recognition. While this is true in most situations, it is especially true here in reference to the single professional. Also, men are more equal than women. And a greying, older father-like man is more equal than any other.

The Single Expatriate Man

Many single men live and work in Indonesia. The launderette and convenience foods of the single lifestyle in the west will be replaced by the services of the wash girl and the cook.

Apart from attracting curiosity over his single status, he usually has few personal problems. Indeed, many young singles themselves say they should be home looking for a nice girl to marry. The fellow seriously looking for wife material may have a social problem, but few have complained about the availability of casual relationships.

The Single Expatriate Woman

While Indonesian women are independent and liberated in many respects, travelling around the world and working on their own as young professionals are not common situations. The young single expatriate woman—even if capable and well trained—may find it difficult to get the status and recognition she deserves. Frequently in this situation, the woman will have a 'back-up' male. Such an alternative was taken by a young woman working in the area of

231

public health. Although she was highly respected by her western colleagues, she found it advantageous to hire an Indonesian male representative to attend meetings with local officials.

The exceptions to this situation are the women who come to Indonesia already conversant with the culture and the language. They can establish their bona fides as friends of the Indonesians and appreciators of the country and culture. That makes it easier to establish themselves as professionals.

PRIVACY

One of the best chronicled areas of distress for foreigners in Asia, not just Indonesia, is the definition of privacy or personal space.

The Western View of Privacy

The typical expatriate needs individual space if he is in a group, and the ability to be physically alone and unobserved in his home. When travelling, one person to a bus seat or bicycle, or four persons in a car is considered civilised. In elevators, it is good manners to demur if it is full. On the beach, in the park, distance is kept between groups of people.

The Indonesian View of Privacy

Keeping in mind that the strongest ethic is one of communal conformity, the Indonesians feel security and comfort in numbers. Privacy is largely a state of mind, not necessarily a physical condition. To be private is equated with being alone, and that is not a desired condition for the Indonesians.

Thus, three to five on a motorcycle is fine; buses are jammed to the gills, but room is always made for one more; beaches and parks are one continuous carpet of people, all interested in each other's activities, and great knots of families and friends move down the streets.

Is There Room for Compromise?

Yes. An expatriate recounted a trip her family took on a local train to a mountain resort. They had arrived at the station early to be sure to get seats. The plan went amuck as more and more people piled in. Each passenger seat seemed to contain first one, then two, then more persons as the train chugged along. Once in the park they felt they had more people hovering round than a banana has fruit flies. It was not a pleasant family outing.

Later, they repeated the trip and from their point of view the whole situation had changed. The train did not seem packed, the picnic was pleasant and relaxed. They felt as part of, but separate from, the group of holiday-makers. It was a pleasant family outing.

What had changed? The situation? Probably not. This is what Dr Kalervo Oberg, an anthropologist interested in the manifestations of culture shock, has to say: '... the environment has not changed. What has changed is your attitude toward it ... you no longer project your discomforts onto the people of the host country and their ways.'

Privacy in Your Home

You have the right to observe your need for privacy in your home. This usually involves working out a routine with the staff. (They are normally very discreet and will give you lots of distance.) Various expatriates have worked out some arrangements. There is neither right nor wrong. Find something reasonable that works and meets your needs.

Some families have the coffee and toast left on a tray outside the bedroom door in the morning. The maid knocks and then disappears. Other families have the evening meal cooked, readied, and left in the kitchen. The wife then takes over and serves as she would back home. Individual *Nyonyas* have informed their maids of their personal schedule for exercise, naps, study or entertaining and the domestic schedule is adjusted for that.

Asians know the westerner needs space and privacy but they cannot read minds: so there has to be some purposeful communication about it. You certainly have a right to the space in your home. Do not make the staff guess what it is.

ACCLIMATISATION QUIZ

If the usual psychological description of culture shock with its phases of euphoria, rejection, accommodation and acceptance seem just a bit too vague for you, we offer an alternative measure for your adjustment. If you say 'yes' to at least half of these statements, you are probably well on your way to being comfortable here.

1. You walk with the gentle Asian swing and no longer hurry.
2. You sleep through the early morning call to prayer.
3. You giggle nervously as you announce to your family that your car had a small accident while you were driving.
4. You ask for more chilli sauce in the restaurant.
5. You spend all night counting bathroom wall tiles and catering to the demands of diarrhoea, then forget to mention it next morning.
6. You sit down to a western formal dinner and wonder why just a bowl, spoon and fork are not adequate.
7. On home leave, you automatically provide packages of tissue paper when people excuse themselves to go to the bathroom.
8. You tell a riotously funny story about the mistakes of an expatriate and neglect to mention it was you.
9. You are faced with a seatless pedestal toilet ... and the footprints that are left on the rim are yours.
10. You prefer open windows to airconditioning in the car.
11. You search the radio dial to find the 'News in Special English' and English is your native tongue!

CULTURE SHOCK RELAPSE

There are bad days (*hari nahas*) that occur with distressing regularity. We just tend not to notice them so much when we are at home.

There are two kinds of bad days for the resident expatriate. The first is cosmic, utterly beyond your control. Bad days of this variety tend to feature major power cuts when you are having 24 to a sit-down dinner and would rather serve airconditioning than food; pummelling rain when the roads and your house roof dissolve along with your patience; being stuck in a traffic jam of marathon proportions and realising that your greatest accomplishment of the day will be just getting home for dinner.

The second kind of bad day is more limited and usually personal. Bad days of this variety tend to reflect physical upset in your office or home. It is when too many *tukangs* (repairmen) are standing around not fixing the toilet which is flushing backwards, or the phone will only ring in when you need to ring out! It is when your driver forgets your address, you are convinced that the power line embraced the tree and shorted out for your personal inconvenience, and you wonder if sweating can be fatal. Stores hang up the CLOSED sign as you approach, and your long-haired lapdog has diarrhoea.

None of these tests for sainthood was designed by Indonesia as personal harrassment. Bad days are *your* problem! The Indonesians call them 'unlucky days' which should be a clue that 'good days' are dumb luck! For the resident expatriate bad days are generally perceived as an assault on sanity.

Bad days are a part of culture shock relapse. They are predictable. They are also often the grist for some wonderfully funny stories, most of which you will wish had happened to someone else.

What's Bad about Bad Days

When things line up to go wrong and frustration, anger and fatigue are at the front of your feelings, the tendency is to take the course of least resistance, accept the whole situation as beyond hope, wrap it up for the emotional garbage heap and label it 'worthless'. The expatriate at this time feels distance from the healthy supports of home and loss of control over his situation; in anger, he sets about to alienate all that is disturbing him. Thus, the dog hides from the wrath of the *Nyonya*, the servants scurry to look for brass to polish, the spouse will be made, if possible, to feel personally responsible for some of the upset, the children will be snarled at and despatched to the care of the TV.

What are the alternatives? Here are random selections of excellent advice from old hands in Indonesia:

1. Avoid dealing with it. If the problem is in the house, get out. Visit a friend, go shopping, get some vigorous exercise.
2. Relinquish control and retreat. If the problem is a cosmic one and the situation is beyond you (do you really think you can impose order on Jakarta's traffic?), cut your losses, rearrange your priorities, change your schedule, take a bath, read a book, take a nap.
3. Keep your friendships intact by not boring everyone with your misery. Acknowledge that the situation is probably temporary, and beyond your control.
4. Avoid major life decisions. Resist hiring/firing household staff, spending large amounts of money, or offering your children as prizes in the Lucky Draw at school.
5. Laugh and be patient.

RE-PROGRAMMING FOR RE-ENTRY

One of life's necessary illusions is that you can always go home again. Indeed, sophisticated communication and transportation can 'get' you home but 'being home' is an emotional issue.

This is not a new phenomenon. Literature is full of the accounts of travellers encountering re-entry problems. Ulysses owed his welcome home to his dog who remembered him; Marco Polo was thrown in jail. We will compare our experiences with those of Master Rip Van Winkle, a character in American literature.

Not all the situations that we discuss will fit each person. The assumption is made that re-entry as described here is a return to the emotional home. Individuals who are retiring, or moving to locations that are new to them, would of course go through all the stages of culture shock. Certain aspects of that are predictable.

GOING HOME!

Why include going home in a book about living overseas? The one thing people living abroad know about *is* home! Observation suggests that people either dismiss the whole question of returning home or assume that home will be the same. Experience suggests that going home successfully means that you have retained certain important emotional and physical aspects of your residency there. For those who have made a successful adjustment here, that is a contradiction in terms.

The day will come when you must say '*Selamat tinggal*' (Peace to you who remain) and return 'home'. Sounds simple, you say. Just call the packers and go. However, that only takes care of your belongings. Your experiences and expectations need some special care from you.

Re-programming yourself for re-entry suggests utilising the same skills and advance planning as moving to a new 'foreign' posting. International media is now giving attention to this phenomenon. Executives are quoted describing their sense of isolation, depression and fatigue from the stress of re-entry. One couple suggested, 'Let's take this (returning home) as though we were moving to a new country.'

What to Do

The process of easing yourself back home is best begun in advance. Each person will construct his own priorities. We suggest items for your list of 'Things to Do'.

1. Educate yourself.

Subscribe to the local paper so that your absence is not measured by your ignorance of local events. Your experiences-soon-to-be-memories-here and your expectations-soon-to-be-occurrences-there need some special care from you.

People refer to embarrassing unfamiliarity with recently famous media personalities, current television stars—the stuff of casual conversation. This is very strongly felt by older children. For this reason, consider subscribing to some of their age-group magazines.

2. Be honest about your feelings.

Are you sad to move? Accept the fact that each family member may have separate and valid responses to the move. (Crying is all right. It relieves emotional stress and allows friends to communicate their feelings, too.) Feelings may change during the departure preparations. Once you have many of the 'leaving' tasks out of the way you may begin to anticipate with pleasure the good things ahead at home.

3. Tidy up one area of your life before moving on to the next.

Make a plan of what needs to be done, and balance that with what you would like to do (and purchase). Keep your plan in a notebook with crucial telephone numbers, dates when the last-minute furniture order can be picked up, and other tasks that must be attended to. You may want to place a favourite servant in a new job, find homes for the family pets, schedule time for lunch with friends.

Do not do too much too fast. Feel satisfied with what you have accomplished so that the business of your life in Indonesia comes to a satisfactory conclusion.

4. Plan ahead to avoid pressures of the last moment.

There may be a round of parties which you were not expecting. These take time and energy you may have scheduled for something else. Even at this time, when your nerves may be a little frazzled, be sensitive to the ways different ethnic groups show emotions.

5. Set realistic expectations for yourself.

It is wonderful to stay in contact with friends made overseas, but letters take time to write. When you return home discretionary time may be at a premium. Don't make rash promises to write weekly when you know you are returning to a life where you are much more than *Nyonya* and *Tuan* ... driver, housemaid, seamstress, handyman, house painter, accountant and cook. Unfulfilled promises will only make you feel guilty.

6. Involve the family in the move if possible.

Each member should have some part in the discussions and in working out the solutions. Perhaps your new house is much smaller than the one you had in Indonesia; let the children work out who will share a room with whom. Consider seriously the emotional value of including the family pet in the move.

7. Begin to re-establish contacts at home.

Allow friends and family the opportunity to form reasonable expectations of you, your lifestyle and values, all of which have changed. Tell them your feelings and expectations (excited, relieved, anxious ... will miss friends, activities ... looking forward to ...).

Recognising the Illusions

Superficial visits for holidays may give the illusion of status quo, but a holiday is not the same as moving back. An often-heard comment from expatriates returning from home leave is that 'Nothing had changed there ... the wives still meet for coffee, etc.' Then you hear, 'I really felt foolish. I went to the bank and found that it had been torn down. I stood and looked at a hole!'

You and your family have grown. Babies and toddlers that came to Indonesia may now be teenagers. Perhaps your children have grown up and away and established a life for themselves in a town which is not home to you. You may have found in past moves

239

that school-related activities helped ease your way into a new community. If you have no children, seek a way through your business, church, or an opportunity as a volunteer to interact with your home community.

Perhaps just the opposite situation will confront you. You started your family overseas and will now have to cope without domestic staff. The wife can start the career she had always wanted but could not pursue overseas. Are the options still open? Will her time overseas be an asset or a liability in this endeavour?

You are physically older. Your child will adore being told, 'My, how you have grown.' Are you ready for 'My, you are greyer,' or 'Golly, you are almost bald!' or 'Put on a few kilos, haven't you?'

Families change, too. The gaps in time will be exposed as everyone catches up on the family news. Families seem to react in a fairly predictable pattern. An often-heard comment is: 'Ah, but of course, that was when you were overseas.' The implication is that 'You went away while we stayed and faced the rise in the price of heating fuel, the coldest winter in a hundred years and endless strikes.'

You may feel that important people in your life—close family and friends—think of your time overseas as an extended holiday. The idea that life overseas is a full-time job for the entire family will not be apparent to them.

The passage of time is perceived differently by people who have been abroad. Perhaps because overseas one's life is a mix of new places and new people, the past at home seems a long time ago. For the people who stay at home, the past was only yesterday.

A long-time expatriate who had not lived in his hometown for eight years returned for a visit. He was greeted by the family barber with a casual, 'Oh, hello, you haven't been in in a while. Been away have you?' The expatriate was disconcerted by the simple dismissal of eight years of his life.

SHARING YOUR EXPERIENCES

'We went back expecting our friends to be only superficially curious about our overseas experience ... The possibility of re-entry stress has been softened by the fact that they have been genuinely interested ...,' a young executive is quoted in the international press. How is this sharing of experiences accomplished? By personal anecdotes, slides and photographs, artifacts, and those ways in which you have integrated your experiences into your life.

People can relate to the commonality of life's experiences but are usually intimidated or repelled by those that are beyond their frame of reference. Remembering that, choose to share experiences that are likely to be accepted.

Choosing Experiences to Share

What is the point of serving an ethnic meal to Uncle Fred? You know that his idea of a gourmet meal is an egg fried tough as a roof tile. Why remark as you are up to your elbows in greasy dishes and fatigued soapsuds that you wish you had your maids with you now? Your two cousins might wonder why in the world they are helping.

If everyone is geared up to take a day trip to the park to picnic and see the tulips, is that the moment to burst into raptures about the orchids in Java?

One returned mother wrote us with the story that her children pleaded with her not to put out their artifacts from their travels. 'Mom, our house looks weird,' they moaned. The living room should not look like the Asian wing of the British Museum, if that is important to the family.

Slowly, Slowly

It will take about six months to be settled. Give everyone time to find a routine. New attitudes need to be established. Experience suggests that after the house and family are physically settled, constructing (or reconstructing) a social and emotional place for

241

yourselves in the family and neighbourhood will take about one year for every three years spent away.

Making It Easier for the Children

Returning 'home' for a child who has never lived there can be a one-way ticket to The Great Unknown. Stories circulate of children who arrived on their home shores speaking several languages except their own!

The issue of schools

Most children raised overseas have attended private schools. Entering a public school system for the first time may be an unnerving experience for them. It is very important that, location and finances allowing, the school truly 'fits' the child. This may mean taking a hard look at continued private schooling rather than the usually less expensive public schools.

From the time a child begins school, the social contacts there take increasing precedence over the family until separation from the family is complete in the late high school years. If the school meets the child's needs, he will probably adjust adequately. Be sensitive to this if the language, sports and socialising skills are not valued in the new school environment.

What good can it do to put the child, who speaks fluent Urdu, Hindi and Malay and is a whiz at rugby, in a school where Spanish is the foreign language and basketball the sport? Instead of being seen as competent and unique, the child runs the risk of being simply weird. School cultures place a high value on being accepted and are quick to exclude the unusual.

Also, if the child has been used to small classes and focused attention from the teachers, finding himself in a class of 30 or more can be discomfiting.

School years begin at different times in different areas. Thus, a move mid-year in one school system could put a child at the very beginning of school term in another, causing the gain or loss of an academic year. If this results in the child being 'put back' it can cause social problems. If the child is 'put forward' the problems can be academic as well as social.

Schools are arenas for 'checking out' new social behaviour, especially for teenagers. The contrast between restrictive and open philosophies, private and public settings, and high and low teacher interest can project some young persons into bewilderment and lost or misplaced values. It is very important for the parents to reaffirm the family values and expectations and provide a frame of reference within which the child can examine the new behaviour.

Research has begun on the experiences of students returning to their home country for university. Experts in the area of cross-cultural living suggest that the best preparation for university is to place the child in boarding school in the home country for the high school experience.

Prior experience is not always useful

Your announcement, 'You've moved lots of times before so this will be easy!' will not serve your children well.

Consider the following: in previous moves from one foreign country to another, there were usually fewer children to meet and befriend; all of them were in the same condition of being newcomers in a foreign country; the resources for activity and entertainment were known and limited; and the responsibility of being representatives of their country was deeply felt by them, helping to give a sense of identity. All of those factors may be changed as the child makes the transition to a school at home.

In addition, many children overseas do not attend their own national school. What of the educational and social dilemmas faced by the Dutch lad who has always attended British schools or the American girl in the French school?

The issue of clothes

A time-honoured way of fitting in is by looking right. The parent who sees only price tags should stifle the urge to outfit the family in Asia's inexpensive clothing or an abundance of ethnic wear. It is better by far to buy most of the clothes upon your return—children will be able to observe the current style.

Reflect that ethnic clothing is great in appropriately ethnic situations but may not score high points in the classroom. In fact, for teenagers to be accepted, research suggests that they should know the current situations not only in dress styles but also in sports, movies, television, advertising, and slang.

Owning your experiences

For teenagers, the appropriate answer to 'How was your vacation' is 'Same old stuff' or 'Bo-ring!' If a teenager announces to his buddies who were bagging groceries that he was camel riding in Rajasthan he would be dismissed as terminally weird.

The challenge to teenagers becomes one of owning and integrating life experiences without allowing these to alienate the people around them.

The issue of maturity

It is often remarked that children raised overseas seem more mature and confident. To support this theory, it has been pointed out that they are *au courant* with international affairs, the complexities of international travel, and participate in the conversations of adults.

To which argument, the teenager in the USA, Canada, the UK or Australia might respond, 'So what! Can you drive a car? Do you know the latest songs? Do you know the local hangouts?'

Mature behaviour becomes a relative issue. What is viewed as mature and desirable by a proud parent might be perceived as an intolerable burden of differentness by the child.

Small children

They take their behavioural cues from the parents. If they continue to feel secure in the presence of their intact family, usually they are all right.

Children raised as infants in Asia have known the intense attention and affection directed at them by the *babu anak* and domestic staff. They might be very lonely for the domestic helpers who cared for and adored them. Take back photographs, picture books, cassettes of music, whatever the child can use as support while these memories are adjusted.

Making It Easier for the Businessman

There is growing research in the United States and Europe on the phenomenon of re-entry stress. According to reports in the media more and more multinational companies are recognising the value of support programmes for their employees.

Dr Bernardo Hirschman, a psychiatrist who specialises in cross-cultural adaptation, remarked in a workshop, 'Living Overseas', that the adjustment for the employed family member is supported by the routine of work. He suggests that some of these persons isolate themselves too much in their work and office and home, leaving the rest of the family to deal with the gritty realities of the new culture—whether this is a new foreign post or a return home. When this happens, the businessman often cannot comprehend the anxiety of the other family members: he feels threatened by their stress as well as helpless to do anything about it.

Career changes

It is human nature to find it easier to grow than to diminish in status. Some professionals encounter difficulty dealing with changed positions as they shift from international to domestic operations.

It is possible that the return home will reflect a major career choice. One professional said he could not afford to stay in Indonesia any longer; if he did he would have accumulated so much specific expertise that it would limit his opportunity for experience and professional growth in any other area. To avoid being professionally limited, he regretfully asked for a transfer.

Making It Easier for the Wife

While the children and the husband adjust in the havens of school and office, the wife is expected to construct the haven for the family, and somewhere in the process meet most of her own needs. A professor at an American college was quoted as saying, 'You don't think that you have any problems, but you do. As a result, you feel a sense of loss and nostalgia.'

Most women can expect, temporarily, a sense of isolation, fatigue and discouragement. Why not? You are, in fact, isolated from the friends you knew best (recently) and suddenly you have a lot of physical work to do.

For some, the change of location is registered emotionally as a true loss and an individual must cycle through all the phases of grief. If this happens, be gentle with yourself and reflect that time will wash the sense of loss from pleasant memories.

Go easy. Realise that you probably cannot do all that you would wish to do for your family. It will take time to get settled so give yourself at least six months before you start evaluating your performance. The same things that gave you a sense of confidence as you settled in Indonesia will serve you now: growing familiarity with the scene, an understanding of how things work, developing friendships, a sense of place—competence.

You will have your memories and personal collection to remind you of your time overseas. Life is a continuum. We all integrate the experiences of the past, but the time to live in is now.

THE RIP VAN WINKLE SYNDROME

There is a lot to be learnt from the charming tale of Rip Van Winkle, written over 100 years ago by the American, Washington Irving. Briefly, it is a story of a lazy loafer-about-town who strolls into the hills and finds himself invited to a party in a time-warp. Rip probably got home later than most party-goers, twenty years late in fact.

As travellers and residents in situations that resemble time-warps, we are concerned with the feelings that Rip encountered upon his return. The story addresses itself smartly with the way we are seen by others. Rip learns a lot, as we can too, from the responses of the village folk to his arrival. Consider these, in the order they are presented in the story:

1. His excitement and anticipation mixed with anxiety (he knew something was different) related to going home.
2. His distress that things are not as they were remembered.
3. People, places, conversations—all factors that are time-in-space signals—are missing or not functioning as they were remembered.
4. The feeling that 'they were strange' changes to '*I* am strange'; remember that while each of us wants to be unique, none wishes to be thought strange!
5. The confusion of slipped identity, lack of confidence in transacting daily affairs.
6. The intervention of a known, credible person in the community makes a place for him in the social scheme of things.
7. Recognition of changed status comes first to the community and then to the individual.
8. Re-assimilation into the community.
9. The experiences become as a story told dispassionately and not too closely associated with the self.

All the quotations that follow are from *Rip Van Winkle* by Washington Irving (Watts, USA, 1966).

As he approached the village he met a number of people, but none whom he knew, which somewhat surprised him, for he had thought himself acquainted with every one in the country round.

It is embarrassing to have to acknowledge too much change. It makes one appear unprepared, out of touch. Memories that have changed become invalid as tools for functioning in the present.

The very village was altered; it was larger and more populous.

Nothing is more boring than hearing someone drone through a list of 'I remember when ...' Quite frankly, who cares? Make the acknowledgement to yourself that a lot of things are different and set about the business of learning how things are now.

Rip called him (the dog) by name, but the cur snarled, showed his teeth and passed on. This was an unkind cut indeed—'My very dog,' sighed poor Rip, 'has forgotten me!'

Each of us wants and needs to be remembered fondly in the past and valued in the present. Shift all of your activities to the present. There are special problems for children who are confronted with relatives they have never met or do not remember. Youngsters are reluctant to be instantly fond of someone they regard as a stranger.

There was, as usual, a crowd of folk about the door, but none that Rip recollected. The very character of the people seemed changed.

Reflect on the stages of culture shock. Persons have to start most relationships more or less from the beginning. One of the areas for frustration and hurt feelings is when the returning family member must invest some time and patience to change his status from guest to functioning family member. In a sense you will have to earn your place again. There are situations where your newness or your experiences can be intimidating.

He doubted his own identity, and whether he was himself or another man ... 'and I'm changed, and I can't tell what's my name, or who I am!'

There are moments of culture shock relapse. Reality for the moment is somewhere else ... memories are rosy and reassuring. They confirm your sense of accomplishment and personal worth in the face of frustration at getting things done—in a situation that should seem familiar to you.

In the story, an aged and venerable man who is an established member of the community comes along and confirms Rip's identity, something Rip was unable to do for himself.

For most, there will be a facilitator in the family or among friends who will ease the way back into the society of the family and the city or neighbourhood. This may be a subtle situation, but usually there is someone who remembers to include you in events and manages to make you sound interesting rather than weird in the introduction.

It may not register with you that initially neighbours greet you as a visitor and not as a resident. You have not been there to maintain your residence qualifications at the personal level.

... company broke up, and returned to more important concerns ...

When the newcomer ceases to be a fascination, he is assimilated and part of the whole.

It was some time before he could get into the regular track of gossip, or could be made to comprehend the strange events that had taken place during his torpor.

Recurring personal memories, whether euphoric or wistful, are your pleasure and pain. But when you get to be a teller of tales as Rip was and your personal adventures are related in dispassionate, third-person terms, you are home free.

CULTURAL QUIZ

The study of other cultures is an enduring fascination. Living in other cultures is an enduring education in self-knowledge.

The moment has arrived when the stage is no longer books and fantasy. You are one of the main characters trying your level best to get along with others.

These cultural quizzes give you a chance to see how you would function in situations that were real for other foreigners here. Most of us endured and thrived with humour intact and a zest for the adventures of tomorrow! There are no hard and fast correct choices. Some are probably a little better than others. Most suggest that a bit of patience, an adoption of the laid-back wait-and-see approach, and the opportunity to see ourselves as others see us will be our best teachers.

SITUATION 1

You have gone to the beach for the weekend. In the meantime the very pampered family cat has run out of dry, sacked catfood. The servants know the pet will not eat rice and fish and thus, on their own initiative, have bought catfood from the supermarket. Unfortunately, the kitchen maid cannot read and she buys a sack of Kitty Litter. When you arrive home you find a hungry, confused cat, and a concerned and upset maid. What do you do?

A Fly into a rage because the cat was fed rocks and threaten to fire the maid forthwith!

B Give in to hysterical laughter and collapse, howling, into a chair.

C Praise the maid lavishly for her initiative and speak to the cat later.

Comments

Your best choice is *C*. It is important to recognise and praise the maid's attempts to care for an animal you value. You would want to wait until she left the room or until she began to smile when you explained she had bought material for the cat's toilet before *you* smile. Otherwise, she will feel *malu* (shame, embarrassment) and that is to be avoided. You can explain the situation later to the cat, who probably is glad just to have you home!

Choice *B* is fine for later but make sure that the maid knows you are not laughing at her. Choice *A* is not even an option.

SITUATION 2

You have been informed by an Indonesian friend of the death of a mutual friend (also Indonesian) several weeks ago. You knew him slightly and his family is in the city. What would be considered correct behaviour?

A Ignore the whole thing since it already happened.

B Send a bouquet of flowers and a card.

C Pay a personal call at your earliest convenience.

Comments

The best choice is *C*. In all circumstances, real points are scored by the personal visit. Choice *B* is all right. Choice *A* is poor form.

SITUATION 3

You have gone with western friends to one of the street *warung* eating stalls. You are feeling adventurous, brave and excited. There are no other foreigners around.

You sit at a table. The waiter gives you the menu, a piece of paper and a pencil and walks away. Does he want your autograph? Do you play tic tac toe? What do you do?

A Write the order yourself.

B Sign your name with a flourish and smile broadly!

C Set up a tic tac toe game and let him have the first turn.

Comments

Choice *A* is a typical method of ordering food in Indonesia. It prevents a mistake being made in the order and allows even an illiterate man to be a waiter. Choice *B* is great after you've written your order! Choice *C* might even work in some situations—but order your meal first.

SITUATION 4

You are in the market with your small children. They are picture pretty with light curly hair and blue eyes. As you walk you find that many people reach out to feel their hair, touch their skin and pinch them on the arm. The children are becoming uneasy, angry and frightened. You know that you should not raise your voice, or point in anger. What do you do?

A Deliver foul looks at everyone and leave immediately.

B Try to explain to people that your children do not like to be fondled and pinched.

C Leave as soon as you can. When you get home, talk to the children about the way Indonesians show affection.

Comments

Actually, your best choice is C but talk to the children *before* you venture into the market or onto the streets. Indonesians adore children, theirs and yours. If your children find the contact truly discomfiting, it is probably better to leave them at home.

Give up on explaining anything. Choice B will not work. Choice A would genuinely confuse the Indonesians who were expressing affection.

SITUATION 5

You are driving in heavy rain. The car floods out and you are stranded. A flock of small boys appear and push the car through the puddle and then surround the car, obviously asking for money. What do you do?

A Yell 'Thank you' gaily, throw coins out the window and drive off.

B Call to the oldest or the obvious leader and give him the equivalent of Rp. 200 for each of the boys who actually pushed and say, '*Bagi-bagi*' (Divide it up!)

Comments

Your best choice is *B*. That means that you have to pay attention to how many boys you have when the pushing starts, otherwise the entire world will line up for payment. Choice *A* is not 'classy' behaviour.

SITUATION 6

You are having an important party. You want to serve grapefruit halves with cherries in the centre as an appetizer. You have tried to communicate this to your cook whose English is as meagre as your Bahasa Indonesia. You use key words—small, round, red—and indicate they are kept in the refrigerator.

You find to your horror that each grapefruit is decorated with bright pink glycerine infant suppositories. The maid is watching for your approval. What do you do?

A Explain to your guests in a quiet voice that the garnishes were a mistake and place yours on a side dish.

B Exclaim 'Oh my God!', grab the dishes from the maid and rush them to the kitchen.

C Have a good laugh and chalk it all up to experience.

Comments

Your best choice is *A* and after the maid leaves the room, enjoy choice *C*. Avoid choice *B*.

SITUATION 7

You check some work done by one of your office staff and find some very simple arithmetic errors that really should not have happened. You are angered and ready to point out in great detail how upset you are about the quality of his work. What do you actually do?

A You inquire if your staff member knows simple arithmetic.

B You burst through the door, point at the employee and in a loud voice ask if he can add.

C You wander in slowly, check to see that the situation is reasonably private and begin with, 'I think we have a problem here ...'

Comments

Opt for choice *C*, wandering in slowly and avoiding a situation of *malu*. Keep the focus impersonal, on the work and not the error and it will probably right itself with no great loss of face. The behaviour in choice *B* is wrong: the noise, pointing finger, loud voice and personal attack. You would not even consider choice *A*.

SITUATION 8

You are not yet familiar with all the stores and you need some airconditioners for your home. You ask an Indonesian businessman, whom you know slightly, for information on airconditioners. You think him very helpful because he asks a lot of questions about your needs.

You find to your astonishment that within days a truck with airconditioners and the workmen to install them arrive to do the work—at no expense to you. This is not what you intended. What do you do?

A Assume that you have stumbled onto something wonderful and plan to inquire about furniture.

B Order the men and machines off the property and lecture them about business ethics.

C Realise that the communication ran into a cultural snarl and send the friend a cheque for what you approximate is the amount of money due.

D Call the person and explain that the situation became confused and that you are not able to accept them as a gift. May you pay? If not, you will have to return the goods.

Comments

Really, you have a choice between *C* and *D*. This situation is common in Indonesia, but it can lead to feelings of obligation that are better avoided. Choice *D* is also an option if the situation comes up in a work context. Choice *A* is not really realistic and choice B would cause confusion.

SITUATION 9

One of your caged tropical birds died in the night. You are advised of that in the morning when its remains are brought in for your inspection. You are appalled and displeased at being shown the carcass. What is going on? What do you do?

A Exclaim 'Oh, yuck!' and scold the gardener for bringing you a dead bird.

B Burst into tears and announce that it was all his fault that your bird died and so on.

C Thank him for showing it to you and ask that it be disposed of properly.

Comments

It is a very strong Indonesian ethic that the *Tuan* and *Nyonya* believe the household staff is truthful. Thus, it is necessary to show the dead bird to prove that it really died. (Of course, if it flew out because the door had been left open accidentally, it might never be reported!)

You may feel that choice *B* is valid, but to avoid *malu* you would not make a public announcement of it. Choice *A* is immature.

SITUATION 10

You meet a pleasant Indonesian woman at a social event and discover to your delight that you live in the same neighbourhood. In a burst of excitement, you invite her to your home and she says she will come tomorrow. You prepare tea and cookies and wait. She does not come. What happened?

A You assume you have said the wrong thing, and spend the afternoon feeling awful, crying, wanting to go home, feeling generally out of place.

B Someone clues you in about the Indonesian 'tomorrow' (*besok-besok*) and you decide to write a book, *Twilight in the Tropics, Tomorrow Never Comes.*

C You decide to give up trying to make friends with Indonesians and join an all-expatriate bowling team.

Comments

Choice *B* is the most reasonable. You may never want to write the book, but you will have learnt that 'tomorrow' is a word that is very, very vague. It can mean tomorrow or never. If you really want to be friends with the woman, call on her first. Choice *A* can cause culture shock relapse. Choice *C* is great if you like to bowl. Do it because you like it, not because you do not like something else!

SITUATION 11

You are enjoying a holiday with your family in one of the parks. Suddenly you are approached by different Indonesians asking that you or your children be included in their photographs. You are not sure how to react. What do you do?

A Accept with pleasure.

B Pretend you do not understand and leave.

C Try to explain why you would rather not do that.

Comments

You select choice *A* or *B*, depending on how you interpret the situation. Indonesians like to take snapshots and often feel they are 'doing honour' by including you. However, it is your privilege to accept or not. A smile and a shake of the head as you walk away is an adequate refusal. Give up choice *C*. Explaining rarely accomplishes much.

SITUATION 12

You are at a social gathering with a mixed group of professionals. You suddenly find that you are being queried about the form of birth control that you use (or do not use). You feel yourself blushing uncontrollably. You do not know what to say. What should you do?

A Answer honestly.

B Answer preposterously.

C Announce that it is really no one's business.

Comments

Either choice *A* or *B* is fine, depending on how you interpret the situation. The Indonesians do not have a vocabulary of tact as in the west for sex and family planning. Besides, birth control is hardly a subtle issue in Indonesia and most people are quite at ease discussing it.

Indonesians thoroughly enjoy the ridiculous response and an answer of 'My husband had a hysterectomy last year' would provoke laughter and also turn the conversation away from you. Choice *C* is irrational.

Bernard T.H. Nopitupuli '85.

SITUATION 13

The maids seem to be hatching a plot to drive you mad. Nothing is ever put away in the same place twice and you are convinced you are losing control. You feel angry, frustrated, and not the mistress of your own home. How do you change the situation?

A Call all the maids together in a group and lecture them on your and their positions in the house.

B Decide your priorities and approach them quietly and systematically.

C Start to follow the maids around, clearing your throat obviously when they do something wrong and smiling broadly when they are correct.

Comments

Your best choice is *B*. Without indicating that you were previously displeased, and avoiding the pronoun 'you', demonstrate to the maids how you want the work done, the items stored, etc. Speak quietly and in private and hope it works.

Choice *A* would cause great *malu* and the maids would begin to look for reasons to leave. Choice *C* would give them lots to talk about in the servants' quarters and probably not change their behaviour!

SITUATION 14

You are the new man in the office and you need to know what the real status ranking is of the expatriate and Indonesian staff in the department. You have been told that everyone has his place and you are trying to figure it out in your section. What do you do?

A Ask the Personnel Office for a list of staff members in the order of their importance.

B Start watching people in the office to figure out the pecking order. Make notes.

C Ask your secretary to write everyone's name in the office for your wife's Christmas and Lebaran card list.

Comments

Choice C is probably your best shot. You have to be casual about asking. She will probably instinctively rank everyone. Choices A and B would certify you as weird.

263

SITUATION 15

During an elegant dinner an Indonesian woman at the table admires your jewellery and announces, 'That is a lovely bracelet. It looks very expensive. How much did you pay?' You are not sure how to respond. What do you do?

A Smile and tell her you stole it.

B Respond that your husband gave it to you and thus it is beyond value!

C Give her a withering glance and inform her that one never asks the price of anything.

Comments

Westerners generally do not discuss the price of something in a social setting. Choice *A* is fine if you make it clear by your tone of voice and smile that you are joking. If it is not delivered as a personal attack, all will enjoy your repartee and the conversation will move on.

Choice *B* is elegant and if your husband is there, may provoke another bracelet from him! Choice *C* is awful.

DO'S, DON'TS AND AN OCCASIONAL WHY

Affection or touching between the sexes is NOT a public event. However, Indonesians of the same sex will typically walk hand in hand or arm in arm.

Anger is best kept in check. Angry noises, angry gestures and temper displays are very offensive to Indonesians and can cause you loss of respect. Work off these emotions with a hard game of tennis or running or squash.

Babies are adored and cherished. Every Indonesian wants to be complimented on his children. Your small children will also have attention lavished on them. Accept this graciously; the affection is genuine.

Bargaining is more than negotiating a discount on purchases. It is primarily a social occasion that is anticipated, shared and enjoyed.

Bathrooms are utilitarian and wet. Educate yourself about water dippers and *mandis* and ceramic footprints before the need arises. Do not expect toilet paper to be provided. Small children should be told what to expect.

Criticism should be avoided! If it must be given, it should be well disguised and very subtle. Criticism is never directed at the individual personally. It is never delivered in public or with observers.

Discretion is appreciated in your public/private life. It is important for the preservation of calm.

Dogs are considered unclean by Muslims but may be pets and/or menu items of some ethnic groups. For many foreigners, they are also pets or guard dogs. They need to be protected against rabies.

Dress. Women should dress modestly and conservatively here. Simple dresses or skirts and blouses with sleeves are recommended. Shorts and strapless tops should be avoided in public. For formal occasions women should not choose extreme fashions or bright colours. For men in business, tropical safari suits or business shirts with a tie are usual today. Shorts are considered only suitable for sports and are not usually worn in public. A *batik* shirt will take you everywhere, worn with comfortable long trousers. A long-sleeved *batik* shirt is acceptable for most formal occasions.

Eating in a family setting is casual and the times are not as set as in the west. Utensils are either the hands or a spoon and fork. Ceremonial eating is often lavish.

Enjoy Indonesia and her people! They like to be told that you like it here.

Feet should never be used as pointers, and should stay off desks and tables. They belong flat on the floor or crossed at the ankles. Bare feet are often preferred for indoors.

Generosity. Indonesians can be extremely generous people especially to those whom they feel are accorded honour.

Getting attention is best done by using some of the Indonesian call words: *mas* (young man), *Pak* (older man) or *Sus* (young woman). Beckon with fingers together in a scooping motion towards you. DO NOT whistle, call 'Hey, you!', bang on dishes, hiss or toot!

Gift giving is a common practice and appreciated. If you are a guest in a home for a meal or a ceremony, a small gift of food or flowers should be given to the hostess or the servant as you enter. Do not expect gifts to be opened or thanks given for them. Indonesians are apt to give what we consider lavish gifts to people they are meeting for the first time. This is part of their honour system.

Hair and hands. The head, especially of a small child, is considered sacred. In general, touching another's hair or head is a major taboo. However, if you have a blonde or red-haired child, Indonesians will delight in feeling and exclaiming over that hair!

Invitations. It is customary to sent wedding reception invitations to everyone remotely connected with the bride and groom. By sending the invitation, proper etiquette has been observed. Indonesians tend not to respond to formal invitations to parties. People here are reluctant to commit themselves to attending an event in the future. (Who knows what will come up between now and then …?)

Language. Many Indonesians speak English well in addition to Dutch, French, German and a myriad other languages. You will be greatly appreciated and supported in your efforts to speak Bahasa Indonesia. Remember: the language is regarded as one of the unifiers of the country.

Laughter is heard frequently. However, it often expresses nervousness, fright, embarrassment, apology, anger, or sadness. Be sensitive to the situation to understand the meaning behind the laughter.

Loudness is for cars, dogs and children! People deal with each other very quietly and speak softly if the topic is important. Indonesians are insulted by loud voices and equate quietness with seriousness and respect.

Names. Say yours clearly! It is acceptable and often necessary to ask an Indonesian to repeat his name. Social etiquette permits you to ask a hostess later for the names of the guests.

Parties. Westerners tend to call every social event a party. For Indonesians, however, most important social events are perceived as ceremonies.

Passing, serving, or receiving is never done with the left hand. It is possible that items will be offered to you by a servant from a stooping or bowing position. Don't panic! He is being respectful.

Patience should be issued with your visa or stay permit! You will receive an appreciative smile and 'thumbs up' from Indonesians when you are calm in any of the 'patience marathons' provoked by the traffic or other urban events.

Paying for a meal is done by the inviter. Going 'Dutch' is not common and considered poor form.

Pinching. Indonesians pinch small children on the cheek and upper arm as a sign of affection. They also pinch harder as a form of chastisement! Do not engage in a debate about which feeling is being conveyed. Do not pinch back. Do alert small children to this gesture.

Please. It is appreciated by Indonesians if you begin sentences that are normally preceded by 'Please' in English with any of the 'gracious words' in Bahasa Indonesia that are discussed in the language section of the text.

Pointing with your forefinger is considered an insult. If you must use a pointing gesture, use your thumb or motion with your chin! Practise at home until it comes naturally.

Pork is an abomination to the Muslims; beef is to the Balinese Hindus. Try to determine the dietary choices of potential dinner guests.

Rice feeds all Indonesians, decorates the hillsides, inspires art and song and is accepted as one of the national unifiers.

Servants are part of the scene here. They know their place and are happy. Foreigners have some trouble with this. It contrasts sharply with their egalitarian approach to personal relations.

Shoes are often left at the door outside a home. Most shoes are biodegradable in monsoon rains!

Sit and stay if you are shown to a seat as an honoured guest. Stifle the urge to give your seat to someone else.

Smile. Indonesians smile a lot. Smile back!

Status is endemic. Everyone has it! It changes with the situation. Your job is to learn how to determine status and to pay honour to those with it—in all situations.

Tense. Don't be! Learn to recognise tension in yourself and deal with it privately. Indonesians will sense tension in you and the situation will become more difficult.

Thank you is most often rendered as *Terima kasih*. This can also mean 'No, thank you.' When in doubt, smile.

Time. Indonesians themselves refer to *jam karet* (rubber time). A 3 p.m. appointment can easily be stretched to 3:30 or 4 p.m. Time is relative. However, it is not acceptable for a foreigner to come late to an appointment. Foreigners are known to be punctual and to be late would be considered rude!

Traffic is a dirty trick. The white line that divides traffic is for foreigners and size rules the road. See also: Patience.

Visiting, dropping in, *mampir*, is something Indonesians do all the time. You, too, are free to drop in unannounced on Indonesian friends. They would be flattered.

BIBLIOGRAPHY

The number of quality books available here on all aspects of Indonesia—history, anthropology, culture, fine arts, religion, textiles—is testimony to the fascination the area holds for people. However, at this point, you can probably do without euphoric testimonies to fascination and move directly to the basics of settling in and functioning.

We have chosen to list books that give you information and encouragement to adopt good health habits; that explain the local food markets and then help you prepare the foods you have bought; that will get you started in the language; and some maps and guide books to make your travels easy.

Getting Serious about Getting Prepared

Several of the books listed are publications of the American Women's Association in Jakarta and have been considered 'standards' by the expatriate community for many years. The books are available to the general public at the AWA Center, Jl. Lauser 12 (Simpruk), Tel: 771947 and at most major bookstores and hotels. The proceeds from AWA book sales go to support Indonesian charities.

Settling in ...

Indonesian Words and Phrases. American Women's Association, Jakarta, P.T. Intermasa, 1989. The newcomer's lifesaver in the sea of new language and sounds. This small book will assist you to say, '*Saya suka ...*' or 'I like ...' until you can fill in the blanks with your own fluency. It covers a basic 'point and name' vocabulary as well as explanations of simple spoken Bahasa Indonesia.

Introducing Indonesia. American Women's Association, Jakarta, P.T. Intermasa, 1988, 5th edition. This guide for settling and living in Jakarta is considered by many newcomers and expatriate residents the 'must have' book for practical assistance in making a home. It is updated regularly.

Shopper's Guide. American Women's Association, Jakarta, T.B. Samaria, 1987, 1st edition. This is a shopping directory for goods and services in Jakarta. It is updated regularly.

A Jakarta Market. Karin Wall, American Women's Association, Jakarta, P.T. Intermasa, 1985. A clearly illustrated, artistically presented guide to the local markets and the food treasures that lurk in them. This was being updated in 1990.

Staying Healthy in Indonesia. American Women's Association, Jakarta, P.T. Intermasa, 1988. This joint project of the AWA and the International Allied Medical Association gives general information about health concerns and provides a guide to medical facilities in Jakarta.

Caring for the Inner Man

The New Art of Indonesian Cooking. Detlef Skrobanek and Suzanne Charle, Times Editions, Singapore 1987. Over 200 recipes are presented combining traditional ingredients and modern cooking methods to give you the best of both worlds in your kitchen.

Foods Galore. American Women's Association, Jakarta, P.T. Intermasa, 1989. A bilingual cookbook especially designed to assist you and your cook create familiar tasting meals using the ingredients available here. The layout features facing pages in simple English and simple Bahasa Indonesia.

Indonesian Food and Cookery. Sri Owen, Jakarta, P.T. Intermasa, 1990. As the title suggests, half the book is information about Indonesian foods, condiments and cooking techniques and the remainder is recipes.

Finding Your Way Around

Historical Sights of Jakarta. Adolf Heuken, SJ, Times Editions, Singapore, 1989. For the person who wants to 'tug at the veil' of Jakarta, this is the book to own. It is well illustrated and clearly written.

Insight Guides and Maps. Apa Publications (HK) Ltd. The Apa stable of travel books and maps is well represented here. Editions of the guide to Indonesia as well as the individual books on Java and Bali are available in German, French, Italian and English. Maps of Sumatra, Java, Sulawesi, Bali, Kalimantan and Irian Jaya are also available.

Indonesian maps. Large wall maps of all areas of Indonesia are published by various companies—P.T. Starnico, Catra Buana, and P.T. Pembina. These large, accurate maps are the ones most often seen in Indonesian offices. They are available in stationery stores, bookstores, and most *pasar swalayan* (supermarkets).

Jakarta Falk Map. Jakarta, P.T. Djambatan, 1990/91, 7th edition. This map makes sense of Jakarta's streets. It is updated frequently.

Times Travel Library. Singapore, Times Editions. These new entries in the travel guide/coffee table art book market are designed to educate with cultural history, guide and clear maps and insider's tips, and delight with stunning photographs. They contain a 'Back of the Book' section crammed with travel notes, best buy suggestions, travel trivia as well as travel essentials. These hard-cover delights fit easily into backpacks, ladies' purses or briefcases. Titles relative to this area are *Jakarta, Yogyakarta, Bali* and *East Kalimantan.*

Getting Help with the Indonesian Language

These books are available at bookstores, hotels, and the book sections of grocery stores. They do not take the place of formal instruction. However, time invested in any of them will give you '*pasar* Bahasa Indonesia' and the confidence to keep going.

How to Master the Indonesian Language. A.M. Alamatsier, Jakarta, Djambatan, 1988, 12th edition. This is the book usually favoured by most Indonesian language teachers. The grammar explanations in English are limited. You will probably find supplementary materials helpful.

Kamus Lengkap. Inggeris-Indonesia, Indonesia-Ingerris. S. Wojowasito and W. Poerwadarminta, Bandung, Hasta, 1980. Westerners speak Inggeris here. This is one of the most popular hand-sized dictionaries.

THE AUTHORS

Cathie Draine and her engineer husband, LeRoy, have been living and working abroad for the last 16 years, 12 of which have been in Indonesia. Their family of three children has grown up in Spain, West Africa and Indonesia.

Cathie's interest in the patterns of adjustment of expatriate families led her to be part of a group that formed a community orientation programme in Jakarta. She is co-editor of two editions of *Introducing Indonesia*, a guide to living in Indonesia and Jakarta, published by the American Women's Association of Jakarta. *Culture Shock Indonesia* grew from her fascination and pleasure in living in Indonesia.

In an effort not to take life too seriously, she volunteers in an informal music programme in the elementary school, goes trekking in Nepal, and worries occasionally about the emotional adjustment of the family's collection of dogs, cats, chickens, owls, turtle and the octogenarian squirrel.

Barbara Hall came to Jakarta with her husband David, a computer consultant, and their four children, in 1979. Culture shock was instant, coming from rural New Zealand to Jakarta.

Barbara worked as a professional family counsellor in Jakarta for several years. As a result of this work, and perceiving how her own family had responded to a new culture, she realised the need for orientation programmes for the newly arrived in Indonesia. She was the originator of the first in-country orientation programme in Jakarta. Later she managed orientation services in Jakarta and in remote locations in Kalimantan, East and Central Java. She has also developed cross-cultural awareness programmes for Indonesians working with foreigners. *Culture Shock Indonesia* is the product of Barbara's belief in sharing knowledge and experiences to promote tolerance and understanding of things that are different.

Barbara and her family enjoy discovering some of the delights of the outer islands of Indonesia sailing on their ocean-going yacht.

INDEX